This series offers the concerned reader basic guidelines and *practical* applications of religion for today's world. Although decidedly Christian in focus and emphasis, the series embraces all denominations and modes of Bible-based belief relevant to our lives today. All volumes in the Steeple series are originals, freshly written to provide a fresh perspective on current—and yet timeless—human dilemmas. This is a series for our times.

Among the books:

Woman in Despair: A Christian Guide to Self-Repair
Elizabeth Rice Handford

How to Read the Bible
James Fischer

Bible Solutions to Problems of Daily Living
James W. Steele

A Book of Devotions for Today's Woman
Frances Carroll

Temptation: How Christians Can Deal with It
Frances Carroll

With God on Your Side: A Guide to Finding Self-Worth Through Total Faith
Doug Manning

Help in Ages Past, Hope for Years to Come: Daily Devotions from the Old Testament
Robert L. Cate

A Daily Key for Today's Christians: 365 Key Texts of the New Testament
William E. Bowles

Walking in the Garden: Inner Peace from the Flowers of God
Paula Connor

How to Bring up Children in the Catholic Faith
Carol and David Powell

Sex in the Bible: An Introduction to What the Scriptures Teach Us About Sexuality
Michael R. Cosby

How to Talk with God Every Day of the Year: A Book of Devotions for Twelve Positive Months
Frances Hunter

God's Conditions for Prosperity: How to Earn the Rewards of Christian Living
Charles Hunter

Pilgrimages: A Guide to the Holy Places of Europe for Today's Traveler
Paul Lambourne Higgins

Journey into the Light: Lessons of Pain and Joy to Renew Your Energy and Strengthen Your Faith
Dorris Blough Murdock

Prentice-Hall International, Inc., *London*
Prentice-Hall of Australia Pty. Limited, *Sydney*
Prentice-Hall Canada Inc., *Toronto*
Prentice-Hall of India Private Limited, *New Delhi*
Prentice-Hall of Japan, Inc., *Tokyo*
Prentice-Hall of Southeast Asia Pte. Ltd., *Singapore*
Whitehall Books Limited, *Wellington, New Zealand*
Editora Prentice-Hall do Brasil Ltda., *Rio de Janeiro*

Frances L. Carroll

Temptation
How Christians Can Deal with It

A SPECTRUM BOOK

Prentice-Hall, Inc., Englewood Cliffs, New Jersey 07632

Library of Congress Cataloging in Publication Data

Carroll, Frances L.
  Temptation : how Christians can deal with it.

  (Steeple books)
  "A Spectrum Book."
  Includes index.
  1. Temptation.   2. Christian life—1960-
I. Title.
BT725.C37 1984   248.4   83.17785
ISBN 0-13-903229-0
ISBN 0-13-903211-8 (pbk.)

*With love and appreciation
this book is dedicated to*

Patsy L. Fleniken,

*who was the first to encourage me
to share my words with others.*

10 9 8 7 6 5 4 3

ISBN 0-13-903229-0

ISBN 0-13-903211-8 {PBK.}

Editorial/production supervision by Norma G. Ledbetter
Cover design by Hal Siegel
Manufacturing buyer: Edward J. Ellis

This book is available at a special discount when ordered in
bulk quantities. Contact Prentice-Hall, Inc., General
Publishing Division, Special Sales, Englewood Cliffs, N.J. 07632.

Contents

Preface

It's all about us! Almost every day of our lives we are confronted with temptation in one form or another. Some of us seem to handle it better than others. It is one of the worst enemies known to man.

Temptation is a matter that must be dealt with as we journey the road of life. For the Christian, temptation is often a bitter foe. Each of us is affected by the subtle manner in which temptation sneaks into our lives. Being made aware of its presence in our lives we must then learn to deal with it. This study proposes to teach you everything you need to know about the subject and then how you can overcome and defeat temptation in your life.

I must confess that as I write this book I feel much like one of the Christians thrown to the lions. The enemy approaches with a hungry look in his eyes, seeking to devour me. The enemy is the Devil. He is very angry with me as I write these words. He wants us to be unaware of his movements throughout the world and be blinded concerning his goals. I feel certain this work will benefit each of us as we learn about temptation, its sources, and cure. It is with guidance from God and with the prayers of many who love Him that we step forward in our study.

I would encourage you to pray before you begin each area of study. If possible, locate some Christian friends who share your interest and study together. Ask God to reveal to you the meaning of the things you do not understand and to open your eyes to receive new insights into the passages we study. Remember, God wants you to know how to handle the struggles of life as well as the victories. He has an important lesson for you to learn through this study and will give you strength when you are uncertain and afraid. You, as a believer, are His child, and He cares greatly for you.

Our textbook for this study will be the Holy Bible, God's Word. We will take a careful look at Scriptures, remembering that His words are true and unchanging. We will apply what we learn in our lives and share it with our friends and loved ones.

Remember, God is greater than any force known by man. He made us in His image, and we are precious to Him. He will be with us throughout eternity

Grateful acknowledgement is given to the following for granting permission to reprint Scripture quotations:

The Holy Bible, New International Version, © 1978, The New York Bible Society. Used by permission of Zondervan Bible Publishers.

The New American Standard Bible, © The Lockman Foundation 1960, 1962, 1963, 1968, 1971, 1972, 1973, 1975, 1977.

The New King James Version. Copyright © 1979, 1980, 1982, Thomas Nelson, Inc., Publishers.

Were it not for the loving prayers of many Christian friends, it would have been impossible for me to complete this book. *Temptation: How Christians Can Deal with It* has not been an easy book to write. It is my sincere belief that it has a great deal to offer the growing Christian.

I thank those friends and prayer partners who have been faithful in praying. Those who prayed have said they sensed the Lord Jesus Christ at work in this project. Several have mentioned they have become aware of the spiritual battle as they prayed. I am grateful for Christians who encourage me and pray for me on a daily basis. This book is a labor of love, dedicated to the loving service of our Lord, in the name of those who serve Him.

A special thanks to my husband, Sandy, and our children, Mary Ann and Ray. Without their daily encouragement and special love my faith and strength in myself would have faltered long ago. Sandy has spent countless hours as my advisor, typist, proofreader, and sounding board for my ideas and thoughts. Our children are wonderful, and they are a continual blessing to me. I am thankful for their notes, hugs, and kisses as well as for their words of encouragement—"Mom, I really believe in what you are doing!"

How can a servant of the Lord fail with so many people standing with her? She cannot! I am blessed to share in the love of Christ with so many precious people.

Agape,
Frances Loftiss Carroll

1
Learning about Temptation

When were you last tempted to do something you knew to be wrong? Something you knew would lead you astray from the teachings of God and would cause you to sidestep His commandments as set forth in the Scriptures? Was it last night, this morning, even now as you read these words? How did you react to the feelings deep within your soul that told you just this once it would be acceptable to give in? Were you willing to do almost anything to gain or do this thing for yourself? Did you feel comfortable when you considered the possible consequences of giving in to this temptation? Were you lured into sin because of this temptation in your life?

There are many questions and ideas for us to consider in our study of temptation. It is a subject not easily avoided in our lives, and one that affects all of us. The battleground of temptation is our mind, body, and spirit. Temptation is a test that exposes our strengths and weaknesses, revealing our hidden desires and showing us the constant need for change.

Don't allow these initial thoughts about temptation to discourage you, for temptation can also bring us closer to God. The focus of our study is to become aware of what we are dealing with in this sensitive area of our lives and then to solve the problem at hand. We don't have to allow temptation to have its way and cause us to fall into sin. We can resist and cast it aside. Temptation can be either an enemy or a friend to the Christian, for in it we can either do its bidding and fall or we can look for God's solution to the problem and be victorious. When we look to God, we understand that He does not want us to be led astray by our own desires, but He wants to follow His directions to escape the nightmare that temptation can cause.

Our task is to become better informed on the subject of temptation. Once we see that temptation comes from our own selfish desires and lusts for gain, then we will understand what it seeks to do in our lives. Temptation seeks to mislead us into wrongdoing. It seeks to satisfy self at any cost. How can we adequately fight temptation and overcome evil in our lives? It can only be beaten by the power of God at work in us. God never allows any temptation to be so strong and overpowering that we cannot resist it. But we have to *want* to fight and defeat the enemy.

Temptation is but one of the numerous battles of life, but one in which we are frequently engaged. None of us has escaped the desires that are brought on by temptation. No matter how great or how small our position in life, we are all tempted. We are all victims of its fiery sting, but we do not have to fall mortally wounded on the battlefield of life.

We are often tempted because we seek something that is just a little beyond our grasp, and we want it. We reach out for it, and it inches away from us. We step closer and closer until we are ready to claim it for our own. We crave to have this thing for ourselves and believe it will satisfy our passions and desires. But it will not! When we take it for our very own, we are trapped; temptation has then resulted in sin.

Some of us like to pretend there is some outside cause for our surrendering to temptation. A popular phrase a few years past was "The Devil made me do it." It's easier to blame the Devil for problems in our life than to own up to our own responsibility. The sad truth is that very often the Devil is not responsible for our temptation at all. It is the self-centered desires of our hearts to gain something we want. Oftentimes that old Devil, as cruel as he is, did not cause the temptation at all. While he delights in helping us from time to time, often he is busy "elsewhere." I do want to point out the fact that the Devil will encourage us along the path of destruction whenever possible. He doesn't want us to overcome evil when it enters our life. We will study more about him and his schemes later.

There is no legitimate reason for any of us to submit to the power of temptation in our lives. As Christian men and women, we have the responsibility to fight back. The Bible has made it clear that we are to resist, fight, and endure when temptation comes our way. To do this we must read the Word of God, study it, and seek God through prayer and meditation. When we are aware of the resources God has for us to use, we can withstand the enemy. You see, God knows our hearts far better than we do. He is aware of our needs for change and alteration in some of our habits. He wants to teach us the way to live godly lives and focus our attention on His will and purposes for our lives. When we learn to do this, our lives will take on greater meaning, and we will learn happiness through serving Him.

For years I did not understand the love that God had for me. Somehow I thought God really wasn't concerned with my life and my problems. It seemed that I was drowning in a sea of temptation and trials with no hope of being saved. I was tempted to steal things when I went shopping, for we lived on a very tight budget and had little of anything. I often considered how easy it would be to slip merchandise into my pocket and leave the store undetected.

Although my sense of fairness and my upbringing knew

that stealing was wrong, I was often lured into this temptation. Only the grace of God kept me from following through and committing a crime. I assure you, it was not my set of standards; I wanted to steal only so that my little baby would have clothes, food, shoes, and so forth. My fairness doctrine and standards were strong only because God helped me overcome. Like most young couples with children, we struggled desperately. There often seemed no way out of the dilemma we were in except to trust the Lord and endure the hardships of life.

When I think back on that time in our lives, I am grateful that the power of God kept me strong. It was a sense of guilt that kept me from falling into this sin. Had I taken something and been caught by the authorities, life would have been a disaster for me. As it was, God helped us to get by and to have the medicines and food we needed for our home. We never starved, but we were often hungry. God taught us that, as we stood strong in Him, we could overcome temptation when it comes, no matter what.

All of us live through some difficult times in our lives. For some of us, we succumb, and our temptation leads us to break the law. Others seem to make it through and turn away from the trial. God does not allow us to enter into a period of temptation in our lives, without providing help. Through every moment of darkness that befalls us, there is a way of escape. God does not allow temptation to overwhelm us automatically. I think the passage found in I Corinthians 10:13 is a prime example of God's reasoning, *No temptation has overtaken you except such as is common to man; but God is faithful, who will not allow you to be tempted beyond what you are able, but with the temptation will also make the way of escape, that you may be able to bear it.**

This thing called temptation is not a rare disease but is something that is common to man. God wants us to know we

---

*I have used the New American Standard version of the Bible throughout, unless otherwise noted.

do not have to be snared by a trap set by evil. He wants us to know how greatly He loves us, how faithful He is toward us at all times, and how much He has His mind set on us. He has given us a way of escape, a way out, that we might turn away and set our mind on other things. God is personally interested in you and me. We need to always remember that He is not some distant God far removed from His people, but that He is a loving, concerned Father to those who will accept His blessings.

I often find that when temptation comes into my life, I want to give in to the thing that lures me into concern only for myself. I don't really want to do what I know God would have me to do. I want to enjoy life to the fullest, grab all the gusto for myself, and have a fling at enjoying life as it is meant to be. When I surrender to this attitude and allow sin or wrongdoing to result, the following things happen:

- I am only <u>temporarily satisfied</u>.
- I <u>want more</u> of the same thing. I am not filled with the happiness I expected.
- I <u>feel guilty</u> for having done something that I knew to be wrong, and yet I know there must still be something that would make me fulfilled.
- I am <u>afraid</u> to face my friends. Although they do not know my temptation has led into sin, I feel they see me differently.
- I am <u>ashamed</u> to seek God and ask forgiveness of my wrong. My mind tells me what I have done is wrong and that God is very unhappy that I did not obey Him.
- I discover that the thing that was so important to me did not really improve my nature or my character. I am <u>still unhappy and empty</u>.
- I am driven for something more. I feel as though I have <u>been cheated</u>, and I want all that is coming to me.
- I find that I <u>envy</u> and often <u>dislike</u> those around me. I look at what someone else has and want the same degree of success.
- I place <u>God in the back of my mind</u> until it is convenient to think about Him.
- I feel <u>uneasy, unhappy with life</u>, and become depressed. I often think I would be better off dead.

Temptation does a great deal to disrupt our spiritual lives. If you made a list similar to mine concerning the areas of your life that are affected by temptation, what would you list? I expect you and I have a lot in common.

HUMAN NATURE

The Bible tells us we have a worldly (natural) nature and a spiritual nature. It is difficult for us to understand how this can be. The worldly nature—our old selves, the way we were before we experienced salvation through Jesus Christ—says, "I am number one. I want my way all the time. I am most important of all." This nature reflects concern only for self and for achieving within one's self all that one believes life to hold. These individuals are self-centered and concerned with becoming all they want to be and with satisfying all the desires of their carnal heart.

In our human nature there is a great desire for certain things. Some of these things become so important, we are willing to do almost anything to achieve them or have them for our own. Some of them are:

- Large sums of money
- Power
- Position within our community
- Cars
- Large homes
- Fame
- An abundance of clothing
- Recognition for our accomplishments
- Desire to accomplish our goals at any cost
- Importance in our work
- Control of something we consider very important in our lives and to others

The list is almost endless as we consider the things the heart seeks for its own. We are never satisfied with what we have, and some of us are driven by the overwhelming desires of the heart. These are things that are not harmful in themselves, but when we are driven to have them, they cause heartaches and problems. None of us knows what drives others to achieve success and a certain control of things in their lives. We are all motivated by something different.

The human nature has little regard for God. It is not especially concerned with what God wants, for it is striving for happiness through its own resources. Our human nature is wrapped up in a form of self-worship and has little time for the things of God. In fact, our human nature has no understanding of God's will or purpose for a happy life. To make this clearer, allow me to explain that God's will for our lives is for us to be happy through Him. When we learn that God has a plan for our lives and can give us the happiness and peace we so desperately seek, then we can begin to understand God.

In our busy world we tend to think we have no time for God. After all, what can God do for us that we cannot do for ourselves? Does that sound familiar to you? We have, seemingly, overlooked the fact that God wants us to live a life filled with thoughts of Him. When we allow God to show us the way to live a God-centered life, things begin to happen. He shows us that the pleasures of this world are only temporary and satisfy just for the moment. But what God has for us lasts throughout eternity.

There is a simple solution to the problems of self-centeredness and worldliness. The answer is Jesus Christ as our Lord and Savior. Locate Romans 12:2 in your Bible. Romans is found in the New Testament after the book of Acts and before the books of I and II Corinthians. *And do not be conformed to this world, but be transformed by the renewing of your mind, that you may prove what is that good and acceptable and perfect will of*

God. Writing out the answers to these questions will help establish these thoughts in your life.

1. What are we warned against in this passage?

_____

_____

2. How do you overcome the problem according to this verse?

_____

_____

3. What are the results seen from the changes, and what is the challenge presented to you in this verse?

_____

_____

4. Why does God consider it important for us to renew our minds into thinking about His will?

_____

_____

God wants you to understand what life is all about. He wants you to pack away all those self-centered and ungodly thoughts and get rid of them. Rid your heart of those things that cause you continual unhappiness, and exchange them for a better way of life. He wants us to find a better way of life and know what it means to receive eternal life through Jesus Christ.

You see, life will never be exactly what you want it to be without the understanding of God in your heart. When you come to God and tell Him you want to follow Him and accept the gifts He has waiting for you, your life will be changed. Instead of seeking fulfillment and happiness within yourself, you will find love. God's love will overflow in your heart, and you will see Him at work. Allow God's love to change the unlovely areas of your life. He will take your ungodly human nature and fill you with a spirit of concern and love for others. He will show you a better way to be filled with the blessing of life when you seek to know Him in a personal way. We talk more about this later, but for now be assured that your old, selfish nature separates you from real peace and happiness.

GODLY NATURE

What is a godly nature? Why is it so important to know God in our hearts? It seems we hear a great deal about the godly nature in our Christian fellowships today. A clear understanding of what it is and what it is to do in our lives is vital to our Christian lives.

The godly nature strives to please God more than man. It is seeking God in the things we do and say as we journey through life. It is God at work in our lives. It is the Holy Spirit that dwells within the Christian, teaching and directing us in the important things that come from God. It is surrendering our old way of life to God, saying, "I know that I have not been able to find the answers I need to life. I give my life to You, that You might direct me along the road of life with a goal in mind. I know You have a better way for me to live. I've tried doing my own thing and have made a terrible mess of things. I don't know what to do with my life anymore."

The godly nature seeks to find out what God desires for us and then follows through, using that plan. God, of course, wants us to exhibit true concern for all people and to love one another from the heart. Loving from the heart is a vital part of our Christian lives; in fact, it is often one of the most neglected areas of our Christian walk.

When we take on the nature God intended us to display as His children, our joy will begin to grow. We are glad to be members of God's family and experience Christ at work in our lives. The more others who knew us before we became Christians see us, the more amazed they are with the changes in our attitudes. As we share our lives and faith, we grow and mature in the knowledge of Christ. When we sow seeds of love, peace, kindness, joy, and happiness, the more others see Christ in us. We are free to express ourselves in a manner we have never known before. Our lives are challenged by various opportunities that God places before us. Although we are still not happy all the time and still have our share of problems, our standards are changed through Christ. We know that when we, as Christian men and women, follow His example, He will respond to our needs. The struggle is placed in His hands, and He sees us through every circumstance. Our strength is in Christ, who shows us the way to walk with Him, in happy times and sad ones too.

Look in the back of your Bible at the book of I John, which is located between the books of II Peter and II John. This short book is packed with power and truth for our lives. *For whatever is born of God overcomes the world; and this is the victory that has overcome the world—our faith. And who is the one who overcomes the world, but he who believes that Jesus is the Son of God?* (I John 5:4, 5). This Scripture teaches us how we can overcome any circumstance that causes us strain and strife. Our task is to be aware of the truth—Christ lives within our hearts. When we fully comprehend this and trust God, then we should fully accept Jesus Christ as Lord and Savior of our lives. Christ has come to overcome the powers of evil and sin in our lives. He is our Friend and Helper, and He gave His life that our sins might be forgiven. Our godly nature should strive to please God in its actions and thoughts. We have received a most precious gift—new life through Jesus Christ. Our task is to pursue it and make the most of it to please our Creator.

WHO IS TEMPTED?

I almost feel like asking, "Who *isn't* tempted?" Every human being on the face of the earth is tempted at various times in his or her life. Temptation is a common occurrence, and none of us are immune to it. Like the common cold, it often occurs when we least expect it. Remember that temptation is not a rare disease, nor should we consider it as incurable. We just need to learn the proper treatment of it, and it will go away.

Some of us seem to experience temptation on a more regular basis than others. It would be wise to closely examine this area to discover why this might be true. Ask yourself the following questions:

- Do I willingly place myself in situations I shouldn't?
- Who do I allow to influence my life?
- Do I fantasize about things and certain desires I have?
- Do I place myself in the wrong atmosphere?
- Do I want to live my life regardless of whom I affect?
- Is there something I want so badly that I'll do anything to get it?
- Do I try to resist things I know to be wrong for me?

These questions will help us to reflect a bit on what we really desire in life. A clear look at our thought patterns often reveals why temptation comes into our lives. We want something we really don't need, or we are driven by a desire that tells us to get a certain thing so that we will be happy.

Temptation comes, oftentimes, because we enjoy the idea of having our own way, no matter how high the cost. Far too many of us are willing to surrender our wills at the first sign of temptation. In fact, some of us enjoy planning along with the various stages of temptation. That is to say, we help it out and submit ourselves to situations we know will only enhance the problem. Instead of resisting the problem, we willingly surrender and wave the white flag of surrender without even the slightest attempt to turn away from wrong when it approaches in our lives.

I hope we now understand what part we can play in our own temptation. I am not trying to make a joke of a very serious matter, but many of us allow temptation to rule our lives without the slightest effort to turn it aside. This can only lead to further temptations, which tend to become more serious each time we surrender. You will experience only temporary satisfaction from allowing temptation to lead you into sin. Temptation always makes our minds and bodies lust for more enjoyment and pleasure, even though we know they are wrong. Temptation given in to leads us away from God, not to Him. Remember, the things of this world will not last throughout eternity. One day we will all have to stand before God and be accountable for our lives.

YOUNG CHILDREN

We might write an entire book on the subject of children and temptation. Recall the days of your childhood, and you will doubtless remember some areas in which you were strongly tempted. Temptation often lures children into unexpected trouble.

When I was a young girl growing up in Tennessee, I always seemed to be into something. I was the classic example of the "tomboy." I loved to climb trees, ride horses, run, and get very dirty. There was a nice, lovely catalpa tree in our back yard, which was my favorite to climb. I would sit up in the tree for long periods of time and watch the clouds drift by like large, white mushrooms. That tree was special to me, and I delighted in cutting out hunks of its bark with a hatchet. Underneath the bark, the tree smelled so very good, and I was fascinated by its beautiful, white wood.

One day my mother had all she could take with my

decorating her tree. "You will not chop one more strip of bark from that tree, young lady!" she said. I knew she meant business. "I want that tree to grow and give shade to our house, and if you chop on it much more, it will die."

My, how I longed to chop on that tree! One day I decided I just had to carve my initials in it with the axe. Finally, when I could stand it no longer, I sneaked out to the toolshed and got the axe. The tree fell victim to my temptation as I carved my initials, FVL. I had a great time doing it and was well-pleased with my work.

I wish I could tell you something dramatic happened to me because of my disobedience. I wasn't the George Washington of Memphis, Tennessee; in fact, I didn't even get caught. One thing did happen, though. I felt very guilty every time I passed that tree and saw my initials. I even tried to rub them off a few times, but they remained there very obvious to anyone who passed by. Even when I was a teenager, that tree still bothered me. I would look at it and wonder why in the world my parents hadn't said something. Surely they saw it. I wonder about it to this day. I don't know if my initials are still visible or if the tree's growth finally erased my handiwork, but I do know I remember the day I was tempted and placed my initials in my favorite tree.

Little temptations, when we succumb to them, can become meaningful experiences in our lives. Nevertheless, guilt somehow seems to remain although the temptation has faded away. Sometimes, the little temptations are as difficult to handle and as strongly remembered as the greater ones. Temptation is something that is always very near and weighs on the mind, even when we try to forget and go on.

Little children are under constant attack from temptation as they grow and develop. They look to their parents for help and support in order that they might know how to deal with many of life's problems. Do you remember how difficult it was for you to handle temptation when you were a child? Seemingly everywhere you went, you were criticized or scolded. Often-times our children experience the same thing.

We seem to fuss and fume more than give counsel and love to our children. Sometimes we criticize them and cut into their little hearts instead of trying to understand and help them. While we seek to help them and give them the proper advice, we often overlook their need to understand why certain things have happened. I for one have been guilty of thinking that children should know what to do in any given circumstance. Our highly sophisticated world tends to forget that children are young and inexperienced. It is our job to help them mold their lives into right standards, not to continually put them down. We need to really listen to our children as they talk to us and speak to them as their friends as well as their parents.

Young children often try their hand at something unusual or strange when temptations come. They might not ordinarily participate in these strange things, but if the setting is right, there is danger ahead. Take, for instance, the child who deliber-ately flushes things down the toilet and stops it up. It may well be there is something more to this act than a mere scientific experiment.

Consider the children who learn how to set up a series of lies to help back up a falsehood. When they discover the plan has not been successful, they tell additional lies to get out of trouble. When they then see the flaw in the story, they seek to cover it over with still more attempts at lying.

Children's minds do not comprehend how parents can dis-tinguish when lies are told. In their own minds, the plan looks flawless, but the reasoning is that of a child. They often have a difficult time dealing with the fact that they have been caught lying and often deny any wrongdoing on their part. Children are frequently tempted to lie and distort issues. We need to help them overcome the need to lie when they feel tempted.

Children who throw temper tantrums to get attention are tempted to do something they know will be unpleasing to the parent. When children use emotions and feelings to arouse other's feelings, we must consider why they are doing so. This behavior is usually an attempt to center the parents' thoughts around their desires for attention. Likewise, children who bite or fight others for attention may be sending out warning signals that there is something they feel that must be noticed by the parents. When children are tempted to hurt someone else to get attention and to use anger or injure someone, the problem needs to be corrected immediately. Temptation is bad enough on its own without it leading to physical harm. It may well be that the child needs added discipline. The Scriptures say much about discipline, and parents are responsible for knowing and applying Biblical principles. We are responsible to train our children in the ways of God. We can't pass that responsibility along to anyone else. Temptation to gain attention or have their own way is very strong in children. The loving Christian parent will guide their child by using Biblical guidelines and help the child to build its life upon these principles.

Young children often begin to face temptation as they first encounter the world through exposure to others in school. The first year or two in school often result in many changes in a young child's life. They are exposed to a world that is very different from their home life. They are tempted by their peers to be like them and to try the things they do, right or wrong. For many children, the battle of being challenged to do wrong by other children begins early. My heart is grateful for the classroom teacher who seeks to teach each child the proper respect and attitude toward others. Were it not for their love of children, many young ones would never learn the value of respecting other people both in the classroom and the community.

Children are tempted to try any number of strange things they know to be wrong. Yet temptation often has its way. We should remind them to seek to do those things that are right and not to do wrong. I am reminded of an event that happened to us one fall. Our son, Ray, wore his new vinyl aviator jacket to school for the first time. He really felt special and looked sharp in his new jacket. That afternoon when he got into the car the tears began to flow. The happiness was gone; someone had stolen his jacket.

It had warmed up at lunch recess, and he took his jacket off and laid it down next to the building in what he thought to be a safe place. When the bell rang, there was no jacket to be found anywhere. Ray's little heart was very sad. Someone had yielded to temptation and taken the jacket.

We alerted the teachers and the principal of the school about Ray's dilemma. Several announcements were made, but nothing turned up. I was angry! I knew the child who had taken the coat was probably wearing it. Surely the family recognized the fact that this jacket was new and did not belong to their child. The child's parents were as guilty as the child in this matter. I gathered it didn't matter to them the child had taken the jacket at all. My only consolation was that the child would be warm throughout the winter.

Before the end of school we made one last attempt to find Ray's jacket. We again made a series of announcements about it. Three days before the end of school, the jacket turned up in the lost and found. The once proud jacket hung like a drab rag. It was badly torn from misuse and wear. Someone had wanted it so badly that he had yielded to the temptation to steal, and now that it was useless returned it. What a sad story.

Still another example of giving in to the wiles of temptation comes to mind. Children do some silly but destructive things when they are challenged or tempted by others. Although there may be a certain degree of humor in a situation, the results can be quite costly and expensive to other people.

While working as a parent volunteer in the public school system of Russellville, one incident really stuck in my mind and everywhere else, as a matter of fact. One day one of the classroom teachers said, "Come here and look at this, you won't believe it." I followed her down the hall to the boys' restroom, where several teachers were peering into the room. Some of the second- and third-grade boys had decided to decorate the restroom with toilet paper.

"It seems," said one of the teachers, "that someone dared one of the boys to wet the toilet paper and throw it on the ceiling. As you can see, it becomes quite an attractive decoration."

As I looked in I saw large blobs of paper on the ceiling. Needless to say, the teachers did not see much humor in the young boys' handiwork. The cleanup job was extensive and took a considerable amount of time. The boys' effort to have fun really wasn't harmless at all.

The temptation of the boys' led them to do wrong, and the results affected everyone. This went on for some while until finally the prank ran its course. The boys were bored and were seeking fun and adventure, but the prank wasn't really harmless at all. Little temptations grow with continual feeding and nourishing; the results lead to sin and additional problems in more than one person's life.

YOUTH

I suppose some of the most common temptations of the youth today are in the areas of

1. Drugs
2. Alcoholic beverages
3. Smoking various plants, weeds, and other assorted things
4. Sexual desires and lust for physical contact
5. Desire to have a position in the social structure in school or the community
6. Desire to be an outstanding personality among peers
7. A need to prove that they are like everyone else.

I expect we have barely scraped the surface of the things our youth are tempted and tried by. It is important to young persons to be accepted in this world today. It is very difficult to be different in today's society. Christian youths are constantly challenged for their beliefs and stances.

"Oh, come on, just give it a try. Just once won't hurt anything! Nobody will ever know and I sure won't tell!" Do those statements sound familiar? They are the same throughout the ages, aren't they?

The battle cry of our world seems to be, "Do your own thing and don't be afraid of getting caught! Just once do what makes you feel good." It sounds like Satan whispering in the ear, doesn't it? It is a dare to the youth of the world, saying, "Don't be different, be just like me." This attitude often leads to trouble, and "being different" is no longer admirable. The do-it-just-once attitude can spoil many of the good things God might be waiting to give the individual. This can lead the one being tempted to a life filled with heartache and lust. Guilt and anger left unresolved in the heart cause an unhappy spirit, and the person can be very miserable until the situation is resolved.

We need to encourage our youth to follow a different pattern from that set by the world. These are confusing years—the growing-up years—and young adults need our love in a special way. Remember, Christian parents, love your children with the love of Christ too, not just with parental love.

Christian youths, especially, need to be listened to. We not only need to be their advisors, but their friends too. They struggle with wanting to be a part of the crowd and yet wanting to follow Christ. Surely we can help these precious youths as they grow and mature in the faith.

Our youths are tempted by evil and pressured by Satan each day of their young lives. What are you doing to help them cope? How are you helping them understand that temptation needs to be met and driven away by the love of Christ in their hearts? Remember, they want to love Jesus, yet they want to have friends and be liked by others.

It tears me up to see how some of our Christian youths treat their peers. They snub and ignore one another because they don't try the same things or hold the same attitudes. These youths have not understood that they share a special bond of love through Christ with all Christians. Surely, we can reach them and have them understand how desperately those of us who love Christ need to treat one another in Christian love.

Our youths should be encouraged not to tear one another apart. Christians need one another for support and encouragement. Reassurance is an important part of our Christian lives. We need to build one another up, not tear one another apart. Even though their views may vary, should not youth respect one another because of what Jesus did for *all* of them on the cross?

Our youths are faced by conflicts of the mind and spirit in almost every area of life. I recall, as a youth, that there were many struggles in my own life. It was a very difficult time for me. The feelings that no one really loved me often filled my heart. Although I had my share of love from the family, my young mind felt no one really cared. That feeling lingered in my heart. Recall the mixture of feelings and emotions you encountered in your youth. How important were your Christian friends?

Showing interest in our young people is never "old fashioned" or out of style. It may well be that a young friend of yours is at a turning point in his or her life and your concern will make a difference. Caring and loving from the heart are attitudes and qualities that are most attractive in a person. We should never neglect those feelings, and we should share them as often as possible. Touching lives in the name of Christ is a beautiful experience and a true expression of love. None of us ever outgrows the need for someone to love us.

ADULTS

Name an adult who doesn't wrestle with temptation in some form? I feel sure there are none! Even the little old lady on the corner is tempted, at times, to do things contrary to God's laws.

The greatest of men, in the eyes of world, does not escape either. Temptation is a common experience. All encounter it, no matter how we tend to deny its existence. As our study progresses we will discuss the various temptations and the methods used to draw us into an encounter.

Adults who believe, "Well, it really won't matter much if I give in this time," or "God doesn't expect me to be good all the time," are sadly mistaken. It *does* matter how we react to temptation as we journey through life. God *is* very concerned about our reactions and attitudes to various situations. It isn't easy to solve our problems within our own power and intelligence; this is why we need the Holy Spirit in our lives.

Christians need to gain control of any temptation that presents a problem to them before it gets out of hand. We need to learn obedience from the Bible and to follow the instructions set before us by its example. Then and only then will we learn to deal with our adversary, the Devil. Remember, if you are a believer in Christ, you belong to Him. He wants you to know happiness and to bless your life through your acceptance of the gift of salvation. We are to learn to resist sin like Christ did because we know Him as Lord and Savior.

Adults, our task is to learn the enemy's battle plan. Now don't think this is a game in which we maneuver around like pieces on a board. Temptation does have a plan of attack, but it is no game. We need to know how to fight it. As we study the Scriptures we will seek the truth from God on how to battle the enemy. God will reveal to us, through our study, what course to follow in fighting the enemy's temptation. Our battle plan is to draw closer to God so that we will not fall into any unexpected traps. Let us determine in our minds to find the truth and set our on our journey wearing the full armor of God.

2

The Purpose of Temptation in Your Life

Temptation is not something to be enjoyed, but it can be viewed as a time of rejoicing in having the love of Christ. As we are tempted, we are given the insight and understanding of how we can overcome it before it defeats us. It can stagger our imagination and dull the senses of our spiritual nature if we are not alert. While we should never seek problems, likewise, we should never overlook the opportunity God presents us to learn through His teachings about any subject.

Temptation wants to steal the spiritual things in our soul by various methods. It seeks to draw us into a state of self-centeredness and separate us from God. It is a carefully laid trap to ensnare our spirits and cause considerable turmoil in our lives. Remember, God never tempts anyone. He does allow temptation to come into our lives that we might be given the opportunity to draw closer to Him and overcome it, but He Himself does not tempt. God says there is no evil in Him and that we who love Him will resist evil. God wants us to know peace in our lives through Him, not turmoil and separation from His love.

God's plan is for us to fight like good soldiers of Christ on the battlefield of life. When we resist and fight, we see temptation for what it is—cowardly and weak. Although this might sound like a mythical battle, it isn't. These things are real. We have ignored temptation picking at our hearts long enough. We need to be informed about it and act promptly. Temptation will not go away and leave you alone until you deal with it. Allow yourself to win victory over the evil temptation causes. It takes effort, but you can do it!

Because Christians believe in Christ and trust Him, why, then, are we still tempted to do evil things? Why have we not been removed from the worry of temptation? The answer is quite simple: Temptation challenges you in the best and the worst of circumstances. Our response denotes our true feelings about our faith and our commitment to the Lord. These are the moments we, as Christians, should permit Christ to work through the problems we face. We need to rely on Christ in us as a continual source of strength.

Temptation is a voice speaking in your heart that seeks to overthrow your daily routine of godly living. It is something that catches your eye. It is a test set before you, looking, examining, peering at you as you really are, not as you wish the world would see you. At times it is designed by Satan to rob you of your joy and excitement as one who knows Jesus Christ. Satan would disrupt and destroy the work of Christ in your life. Temptation is often devised by Satan to throw you off track and confuse your life. When viewed properly, it can be overcome and can lift your spirit. God will allow it to build your faith into a more mature and secure structure as you turn temptation after temptation aside.

When a Christian is faced with temptation and trials, they must first recognize the problem for what it is—an outside

bySATAN

attempt to disrupt your peaceful spirit. It seeks to deceive you by telling you there is more to life than what you have. The deceiver—whether the Devil or the lusts of your own heart—seeks to show you a better way; that way is pleasing to the old nature. Temptation can make you sway in the wind like a shock of wheat, tossed to and fro. It will toss, push, and bend you in various directions until finally something happens:

- You break, falling from temptation into sin.
- You bend the rules to fit your own needs and forget about God.
- You become firmly rooted and take a stand in Christ.
- You learn to endure, holding onto the promises of Jesus that assure you He will never leave you or forsake you, never.
- You stand and resist the temptation in the name of Jesus, and it will retreat.

God allows us to be tempted that we might discover our need to be enriched and strengthened through Scripture reading, praying, and meditating on the example set by Jesus Christ. God always has a way of escape available for those who trust Him and seek His guidance. We merely need to seek the answers He has for our situation. God supplies us with solutions; He helps us open the right door and see it for ourselves. The answer will not come without us looking for help and seeking His will for our lives. We must *want* to find it.

Temptation also comes that we might discover God has a better way of life, one filled with meaning for those who love Him. We should be ready to fight the enemy as he entices us. Temptation seeks to cause our hearts to be led into disobedience and to turn away from God. God's Word says it need not be that way. Know to whom you belong, then look to God for all things. The enemy uses temptation to get our attention from God and focus on ourselves. It either drives us from or brings us to God, depending on our reaction to it.

WHAT TEMPTATION DOES

Notice that I write of temptation almost as an opportunity. Temptation can be a builder or a destroyer, depending on our response to it. It can tear down our godly nature if we continually give in to it. It will eat away like a cancer until it takes all the beautiful things in our life and makes them ungodly and ugly. It will take a content heart and turn it into a hardened heart, self-seeking and wanting for itself alone. We alone control what decisions we make.

When used as a builder, temptation can cause the Christian spirit to grow in knowledge of the Word of God. Temptation will clearly point out the need for a daily walk with Christ. Temptation, when handled through our ultimate source—Christ—will be turned into victory. The victory comes as temptation is resisted and turned away, and we walk on stronger in faith. We know we did not surrender to evil and are glad.

How often have you felt, "Just this once, and I won't ever do it again. Nobody's perfect! God doesn't expect me to be sinless all the time," and give in to temptation? Temptation is our human nature and our spiritual nature at war with each other. The victor is the one who realizes this and knows that temptation is not uncommon. All have been beaten down by its angry blows at some point in life. It is in dealing with it that we understand God has a better way of life. The more we learn about God's way of living, the more He will reveal Himself to us.

As we view temptation in our life, what are the benefits of having to face various problems?

_____

_____

_____

TEMPTATION YIELDED TO

In most of our lives, temptation is more common than the flu. All are affected by it. Make a list of the various kinds of people by their professions, who might face temptation. List those who face the most temptation at the top of your list.

1. _____

2. _____

3. _____

4. _____

5. _____

6. _____

7. _____

8. _____

9. _____

10. _____

There seems to be a worldwide dilemma, doesn't there? It sneaks up on the foot soldier, the ruler of a nation, the vagabond, the prominent socialite, the financial wizard, the minister, the housewife, the teacher, the child, the senator, and even the President. None are immune to the disease of temptation. The battle is at hand, and we must all decide what to do.

What brings temptation into our lives? As far as I know, there is no key to unlock the mystery of why and how the victim is chosen. It may well be we are lonely and depressed. These emotions often make us feel unlovely and unloved. As temptation arises, it may make us feel like we are the most important person in the world. Temptation is sneaky and cunning.

Maybe you have just experienced a mountain-top experience and feel success and happiness in your heart. Something you have experienced has brought you great joy and pleasure. Temptation enters the room saying, "I can give you more!" When we least expect it, temptation is always close at hand, ready to deal out a double dose of joy and pleasure, which, when accepted, quickly becomes a double dose of struggle and heartache.

It has been my experience that I am tempted most when I am tired, very tired, and almost always when I am alone and bored. At such times my guard is down, and my body and spirit seem weary. I am then receptive to the negative instead of the positive in my life. It is at these moments that I want to go off somewhere and get away from the hectic world around me. Then temptation hits . . . full force!

When temptation enters, it says, "You know, it really isn't all that important to follow God's will all the time. After all, nobody will ever know, and you will feel a lot better and be happier that you gave in this once. You know you'll never have another chance, so take it now!" The temptation continues to grow and tries to consume my spirit and tempt my mind. It is difficult to reason, and I feel drawn toward the temptation. I do want to have some "real fun" for once, and it seems very important at the moment.

When I am tempted I am almost never drawn to God. The fact is, I tend to forget all about God. It seems my friends are very far away and have forgotten me. At these times I wonder if I even have friends who care—the children don't seem to love me, neither does my husband or anyone else—temptation has me badly deceived. It has a real foothold on me now and is about to shut the door of reality behind me. I am almost trapped in an inward room of darkness and doubt.

Have you ever noticed that, when you are tempted, there seems to be no answers immediately available, let alone the knowledge of how to get out of it? I must make a decision either to follow the temptation or to take a stand. To take a stand takes effort and willpower. If I say yes to temptation, there will be a brief encounter with temptation, which will result in sin. The pleasure will last but a short while, but the guilt will linger in my heart. What am I to do?

When temptation comes, it must be put aside or it will grow and cause sin. The decision is ours. We must determine what we want in life and who we want to control our life. I can almost hear you say, "Ah, come on now! It doesn't have to be that way, choosing either good or bad." Friends, there isn't any ground in between. We have to make a life-changing decision each time temptation erupts in our life. Choosing good brings light; chosing bad brings death, darkness, and despair to our spiritual life.

When temptation is not put aside, something always happens. The choice is in our hands and on our hearts. I hope we choose wisely.

TRUTHS ABOUT TEMPTATION

There are certain truths we must recognize in order to deal with temptation effectively. Let's look at them briefly and consider them under God's direction. Underline the words below that speak to your heart on the subject of temptation in your life. Don't skip them, for each word is important and will give you a foundation upon which you can begin to build a happier life. Pray and ask God to reveal important truths to you as you study.

- All are tempted; some more than others.
- Temptation can be a supernatural experience or can be humanly triggered.

- Temptation is one of the major battles the Christian faces.
- Temptation is strong, but not something that cannot be overcome. We must learn to resist and flee the forces of evil when they first appear.
- Temptation can come from your own desires and heart as well as from the Devil.
- Temptation given in to will return to haunt you. Each time you do not resist the temptation, it will grow stronger and return.
- No temptation is stronger than the loving power of the Lord Jesus Christ.
- Temptation is not a permanent defeat in your life. It is merely a small part of the maturing process.
- How you handle the various temptations in your life will very often affect you mentally, spiritually, and physically.
- God seeks for you to draw closer to Him when tempted. When you see that you cannot handle problems alone, God will be faithful to help you through the most adverse of struggles.
- Our Lord Jesus Christ never abandons those who believe in Him. Jesus freed us from the power of sin to destroy and claim our lives. Our gift of salvation has set us free, and we are forgiven. Jesus took your sins and mine to the cross, so that evil would have no claim on us. His gift has given us new life through Him. (That's good news for those who believe and accept it as it is—a gift called salvation.)
- Temptation is only temporary. It will either determine your faith in Christ as genuine or disprove your trust in Him. Christ will not allow temptation to overtake us if we follow Him.

The lessons learned during the hours of temptation can make a changeable difference in how you decide to live your life. Temptation is often brought into our lives by the desire for something we feel we really want or need very much. We are usually unable to envision the long-range effect it may have on our lives. Allowing this desire to rule our heart results in sin. Sin causes us to become separated from the good things which are of God. Sin causes God to turn away from us, for He cannot look lightly upon sin.

Describe how you feel after you have become a victim of temptation and have fallen into some kind of sin.

_____

_____

_____

At this moment, what are your personal feelings about God? About yourself?

_____

_____

_____

Many of us have not understood the Christian walk with Jesus as a vital part of our lives. One step at a time is all Jesus asks us to take as we travel the road of life. We have to choose with whom we will travel through life—Jesus Christ or that old Devil, Satan. With Jesus, we will have a loving Companion; with Satan, we will have despair and darkness.

What does your heart say to you this moment about the decision at hand?

Our Christian walk is filled with hope and eternal promises from God our Father. We will not lose the way or choose the wrong road. Although we become confused and struggle from time to time, the Holy Spirit is with us and will not forsake us. Jesus allows us to make our own judgments and decisions. He wants to be a strong part of our lives and show us a better way to live each day of our lives. He doesn't force His love on us, however, but waits until we are ready to receive it. Allow me to say at this point that we cannot measure His perfect love in human terms; it is limitless. I know of nothing as wonderful as the agape love that comes from Him into my life.

As we are tempted and tried, He displays His love for us. As we struggle and encounter our enemies, He stands as our Protector and King of hope. Without Jesus in our lives, the struggle would be far more difficult to overcome, for evil would finally consume our spiritual nature, and our hearts would become hardened to all that is of God. With Jesus in our lives, we know to whom we belong and in whom we can place our complete trust. Jesus will help us overcome and guide us along the pathway of life.

3
Kinds of Temptation

When you think of temptation in your life, what words best describe the power it has over you? Shady, enticing, fascinating, attractive, or perhaps inviting are a few of the words that describe the various lures to be led astray. To join with these colorful words are a multitude of temptations that enter our lives. Let's consider for a few moments the kinds of temptations that enter our hearts and that must be dealt with.

Fleshly	*Worldly*	*Spiritual*
drugs	social status	worship of Satan
laziness	larger homes	desire for things
abnormal sexual	fame	without a real need
desires	money and riches	for them
smoking—habitual	position in business	worship of other
drinking	cars	persons
overeating	travel for the sake	abnormal pride or
self-worship of	of showing or impressing	adoration of self
one's own body	others	

Fleshly	*Worldly*	*Spiritual*
gossip	an overabundance of	lack of need for a
ego	clothing to impress	time of worship
	others	no need to read or
		study the Word of
		God
		seeking of super-high
		religious experiences

As you see, we have barely touched the tip of the iceberg of temptation. There are many things that lure us into trouble. The most valuable information I can share with you on the subject is that anything that seeks to continually draw you from the realm of God's standards is temptation of a sort.

We will consider a few of these areas of temptation, from the biblical view, as well as from common sense reasoning. When a person seeks to gain possession of something so desperately that they are overwhelmed by the need to have it, temptation has taken root and is growing. Many of us are lured by a compulsion for a special car to fill our driveway. We see the beautiful car gleaming in the sunlight. As we settle in behind the wheel, we feel "great." The power under the hood of the automobile sends us gliding along the highways and byways of life. This car, somehow, becomes a part of us and makes us feel special. We are drawn to it like a moth to light. We must have it for our very own. We are lured into the trap.

I realize some of you think this is an impossible situation, but it is very real. I can almost hear you say, "How could anybody find any car that attractive?" Well, friends, stranger things have happened in this world. Each of us has our own special weakness. Satan knows how to draw us to the desire of our heart. Remember, our human nature says, "Me first."

For some of us the driving temptation of our lives is to gain a super-high religious experience each time we assemble in the church. Temptations are often spiritual in nature. We should ask ourselves how we should experience the Holy Spirit at work in our lives? When we are driven to have many supernatural experiences and desires, we can be tempted to give way to our emotions. At times, we tend to allow emotions to rule our entire thought process. While our religious experience should be a time of happiness and communication between our spirit and the Spirit of the Lord, it should not be a time of deliberately working ourselves up into an emotional frenzy to distort our view of the message of Christ. I see the Christian life as a constant walk with the Lord, having highs and lows. Our spiritual walk involves an equal balance of mind, body, and spirit. In worship experiences, it is not self-gratification we should seek but the enrichment of our lives through a personal knowledge of Christ. Uncontrollable emotions can distort the true light of Jesus Christ. Emotions often allow shadows to affect our perspective and shift our attention to experience, thereby minimizing our focus on God's Word. Many of our modern-day Christians tend to think of their religious experience as supernatural. The trend is to say, "Look at me, see what Christ has done in my life. Why haven't you experienced it too?" Christianity is a faith that speaks first of Christ, then of helping and serving others, placing ourselves last. We should turn from some of the extreme emotionalisms, with the understanding that Christianity is not a sideshow; it is a steady, consistent walk with Christ. The person who seeks to be up front or center stage all the time may have a problem dealing with what is of prime importance—self or Jesus.

I think a close examination will reveal much of the truth about some so-called super Christians. Even the greatest religious teachers and ministers of today seek to shun the spotlight. They know Christianity is not a fantasy religion with staged performances along the way, but a genuine feeling of love and confidence in Christ. It is putting Christ first in all things and allowing Him to direct one's steps. It is a faith that is meant to serve others. There is no room for glorifying self. Jesus taught the people that He came not to be served but to serve. Jesus was always consistent and clear in His teaching.

Still another example of temptation is the competitive seeking of a position that will advance your career. This can be one of the driving factors in your life and can cause great problems if not handled through Christ. Those of you who are involved in the daily work process know how "humdrum" a job can be. None of us are really content to stay in the same place, but we seek a better opportunity in life. As we often tire of the daily routine and allow ourselves to think ahead to the next step up the ladder, we can begin to scheme and plan how to get ahead of others. In the job force, the competition is always stiff. The real battle of survival often seems won by the fittest or the one most clever at deception.

The spirit of competition remains strong in today's world. We struggle and wrestle with ideas of how to get what we want. Temptation whispers in our ear and says, "Step on anyone you have to, to get your way. Don't look back. It's important for you to get ahead. Life will be better for you when you are the boss." Temptation always knows what to say to set us reeling. Unless we are keen to the Holy Spirit, who tells us how to stand strong, we can drift off course.

When struggling for a competitive promotion, we can be tempted to ignore brotherly love. Temptation often places friend against friend to vie for the same job or position. If not watched carefully, problems will tend to destroy even the deepest of friendships. Somehow you feel you need the position more than your friend. You seek to influence the boss in some manner. Maybe a rumor or two will take your friend out of the running for the job. After all, you have more education and experience than your friend, and you really do want the job very much.

You will note how temptation always seeks to please itself. You know you have a right to make a claim on that head clerk's job, and you take the steps necessary to be noticed. Strange things happen as we become overpowered by a desire of the carnal heart. Nothing will humanly satisfy us. We must gain control of this position. However, if we do gain it, we still always seem to want more.

Why is it important to concentrate our thoughts toward refuting temptation when it comes? Why should we continue to negate its powers? The answer is really quite simple: So that it might not rob us of our joy and peace in Christ. There is much to lose by allowing temptation to lead us into continual sin. Let's concentrate on what lies ahead when we continually sin.

Journey with me on a Biblical safari to learn for yourself what God has said on the subject. The book of I Corinthians is located almost one-third of the way into the New Testament, after Romans. Chapter 6, verses 9 thourgh 12, bears the undistorted Word of God and a caution to the danger ahead for those who think God has no plan for the future. *Or do you not know that the unrighteous shall not inherit the kingdom of God? Do not be deceived; neither fornicators, not idolaters, nor adulterers, nor effeminate, nor homosexuals, nor thieves, nor the covetous, nor drunkards, nor revilers, nor swindlers, shall inherit the kingdom of God. And such were some of you; but you were washed, but you were sanctified, but you were justified in the name of the Lord Jesus Christ, and in the Spirit of our God.*

In these verses are mentioned the many areas of our lives in which we are often tempted. And what is it the Apostle Paul says? *Those that do these things shall not inherit the kingdom of God.* What a blow to our ego! But then his words continue to speak to our hearts, saying, *When you lay those things aside in your life and turn to Christ, you are forgiven and cleansed of these sins.* What a joy! We can be forgiven through Christ and receive an inheritance in the kingdom of God. What greater blessing could we desire? God considers us special to reward us so graciously.

For those enticed in the sexual realm, the roots of their problem run deep. While the mind tells them that the beautiful creature who has caught their eye is luscious and appealing, God clearly says, "no!" Satan's insidious plan is to dull our senses in order to seduce us into pleasing our lust for fleshly satisfaction. Satan often uses sexual desires to draw us away from God's plan for our lives. The sexual drive does peculiar things to our senses.

It isn't a pretty picture, is it? We know that God forbids casual sexual relationships, but yet they fascinate and stimulate the mind and body. Recall Romans 14:12: *So then each one of us shall give account of himself to God.* We will at some time in the future stand before God in judgment. We will be called upon to explain our actions and attitudes for today. We should give serious consideration to how we will respond to God's judgment as we stand before His throne. I fear we will be dumbfounded and unable to answer, for our excuses will be revealed as nothing more than attempts to conceal sin.

Be aware that Satan is seeking to mislead and dupe you by stating that beyond this life there is nothing more. He will swear there is no eternity, or heaven, or hell, with either God or Satan. All there is for you is today, so Satan will say. Satan lies! God has told you the truth. We have a choice to make. With whom will we spend eternity? We must make that decision as we live today, not after we die. Our lives are filled with today, tomorrow, and eternity. I hope you have chosen God's way.

In I Corinthians 3:16, 17 is stated another truth which I believe is very important. When I first learned it in 1976, I was a very young and immature Christian. At that point I had become miserable and unlovable in many areas of my life. Suicide often entered my mind, and I felt no reason to live another day. One afternoon in total desperation I sat on the side of the bed, pistol in hand, pointed to my head, and ready to fire. I thought and thought about what I was about to do. Surely there must be a better way of life than what I knew now. I could almost hear the Devil laugh, "Go ahead, pull the trigger. You know there is no one who cares for you and things will never be better!" I could feel his nastiness and bitterness all about me. His presence was very real at that moment in my life.

Finally, in total desperation I laid the gun down on the bed, fell to my knees and shouted, "God, if You really are and really exist, do *something! Anything!* I can't go on like this anymore. I want to die; give me something to live for." I was tormented in mind and spirit with no way out. I didn't really want to die, but I didn't want to live either.

I was miserable, almost without hope, and then I felt an awareness of God within me. "Frances, do not do this thing. Put the gun away and turn your life over to Me. I have many things for you to do for Me. You must change your ways and follow Me. Prepare yourself to follow after Me. Your life belongs to Me, and I have numerous things to teach you that you might serve Me and be My child." A strange peace began to take hold of me. Although I did not have the answers, I knew God cared, even if I thought no one else did.

A few days later, I actually opened a Bible and began to read it for the first time in many years. As I read I Corinthians, a verse in chapter 3 spoke to me. I read, *Do you not know that you are a temple of God, and that the Spirit of God dwells in you?* (v. 16). No, I did not know! *If any man destroys the temple of God, God will destroy him, for the temple of God is holy, and that is what you are* (v. 17). I was flabbergasted to think a part of God actually lived in *me.* I had to stop and think this one over for a while. I didn't want to dishonor God. I discovered it really mattered to me to know God personally.

I began to reason, "If God lives in me, I have treated Him rather shabbily. If God lives in me, why does He? What does it really mean? If God loves me enough to live in me, how should I live?" These were questions I had no answers to, and I wanted to understand. God began to show me how I had really made a mess of my life. I hadn't been the kind of person that I knew I should be. Sure I was a Christian, at my own convenience and leisure, but not at His calling. Just how could I learn to be what God wanted me to be? What would I have to do? How much would I have to surrender in my life?

As I looked at my life, certain truths began to emerge. I

had very little going for me at this point in my life. To look for what God had to offer would only make life better, for it seemed like hell on earth now. It seemed that whatever I gave up God would replace with something far better. Thus, I reasoned, I will surely be happier than I was today. I discovered that I mainly needed to change my temperament and my selfish attitudes. I didn't have room to love anyone because I cared only for myself. I needed to learn to love and accept others as they were, not as I desired them to be.

The kingdom of God does not consist of words but of the power of God. God very quickly taught me many lessons about changing my attitudes and seeking goals in life. I needed not to depend on myself but rather to draw on the power of God to show me how to do the things I needed to do. God soon taught me how to be sincere of heart. He impressed me with the necessity of caring and loving others as He loves them. He directed my spirit to a deeper understanding of love than I had ever known before. I discovered I should offer myself to others by sharing my abilities and gifts. Most of all, He showed me that true Christian love has "no strings attached," and that I should give of myself for the joy of sharing what God has given me not for what I want or expect in return.

I know what temptation is in the life of an unbeliever and a believer. I have experienced the desperation of the heart and soul that seek a better way of life. Temptation has placed stumbling blocks in my path, many times seeking to cause me harm. It has even tried to persuade me that there is no need for God, but now I know differently. Temptation to the point of looking death and the Devil in the face has caused me to draw closer to the One who loves me—the Lord Jesus Christ. I learned that temptation can even lead to destructive deeds of the heart. I also found out that Christ wants to take our weak points and change them to strengthen us. Temptation can reveal the power of God in your life and how He will overcome, if you will seek God.

Our worldly system becomes more corrupt with each passing day. It would tell us that doing whatever we desire in our heart is good, that there is no wrong. The Scriptures advise us that we must make a decision concerning which course to follow. In I Corinthians 10:21 there is a simple truth for us. Flip over a few pages and find it. *You cannot drink the cup of the Lord and the cup of demons; you cannot partake of the table of the Lord and the table of demons.* You see, we are told by this verse to make a decision. When temptation moves in and pulls us away from the protection of Christ, it weakens our spiritual nature. Whatever the allurement is, whatever thoughts you have, wherever you go, it will separate you from the good in your life.

Have you noticed how temptation sneaks in and out of your community? When someone gets something their neighbor doesn't have, soon the desires begin to grow and fester. Pretty soon the desire festers like a ripened sore until something has to be done to relieve it. Someone decides it is time to treat the sore. The only problem is, they use the wrong medicine. We doctor the sore of temptation instead of seeking to cure it. We allow temptation to have its way, which results in infecting instead of healing the sore.

Allow me to make this illustration a bit clearer. Communities and neighborhoods often take on certain personalities and social traits. For a while our neighborhood was tempted by an epidemic of people adding on rooms and building fireplaces. Pretty soon we were all talking about fireplaces and wanting them in our homes. It seemed like a fantastic idea, and, after all, other people have them, so let's have one! One nice thing about some temptations, they add a lot to our style of living. Fireplaces smell great too! Everyone wants their home to be comfortable and stylish. Unfortunately, I just get to smell the neighbors' wood burning. We don't have a fireplace yet, but we are still thinking about it. And on and on it goes.

Some of us are tempted into wanting nice things, sometimes justly. We all like nice things. The trick is that we must learn how to be careful about the things we desire and not to allow them to rule our heart. Some things in moderation are not bad for us. Often it's how we respond to what we get that counts. <u>God does want us to have nice things and be happy, but not at the expense of forgetting about Him</u>.

I suppose, at this point, we should talk a few moments about our friendships and companions. Turn once again to I Corinthians. This stop will be made in chapter 15, verse 33, which reads, *Do not be deceived: "Bad company corrupts good morals."* What kind of company do you keep? Who are your friends? Are you in the companionship of those who seek only the best God can give for you? What is their language like? How do you feel when you are with them? Do they arouse suspicion in your thoughts about them? Do they gossip, lie, cheat, drink excessively, indulge in abnormal sexual activities? Just who are your real friends?

1. List three of your good friends.

   _____

   _____

2. What do you like most about them?

   _____

   _____

3. What do you really have in common with them?

   _____

   _____

4. Are they Christians?

   _____

   _____

5. Is there any one of the three with whom you feel the most comfortable? Why?

_____

_____

_____

6. What do you talk about when you are with these people?

_____

_____

_____

7. How far do you go in trusting your closest friend?

_____

_____

8. What would you change in the personality of your closest friend?

_____

_____

9. What does your best friend think of God?

_____

_____

10. Are you happy with the friendships you have in your life at present? Why or why not?

_____

_____

_____

The method we use to select our friends and companions is important. The Bible says that we are known by the fruit we bear. Whether we do good or bad does matter, and our friends tend to have a strong influence on us. When our friends are firmly grounded in the knowledge of God, we tend to be in tune with God too. If our friends are hell raisers, corrupt, and have a loose living style, they usually try to have us follow the same pattern.

What does all this mean? What does God's Word say about our relationships with others? Turn to II Corinthians 6:14, 15. Make a list of the things you consider to be important in these two verses. It won't be difficult to locate 2 Corinthians in your Bible, look just before Galatians and after I Corinthians.

Do not _____

_____

_____

_____

What is it Paul would have us do in our Christian life? Read Ephesians 4:1-3 and fill in the blanks in the following statement. (Look for Ephesians in the New Testament before Philippians and after Galatians.)

Walk _____ *with*

_____ *with all* _____

and _____, *with* _____

_____

_____ .

Choose your friends well. Be concerned with their attitudes and their spiritual condition. Whenever possible, seek those who are in Christ. There is a special bond among those who share the love of Christ in their hearts. There is a special spiritual unity in having friends who know Christ as you do and who can share ideas with you. You need not be as skeptical of them as you might be of those who do not love Christ. Experience the peace, joy, and contentment that comes from sharing with others who have spiritual knowledge and understanding of faith in Christ. Isn't it wonderful to have friends who can share in these attitudes!

Let's look for a minute at the importance placed on this area of our life. Philippians 2:1-5 lists several feelings and attitudes we should have toward those who are in fellowship with Christ.

1. Look at the verses and list what you find.

   a. _____

   b. _____

   c. _____

   d. _____

   e. _____

   f. _____

   g. _____

   h. _____

2. According to verse 3, how are we to regard one another?

   _____

Do you see the importance of Christian friends? When you consider someone as more important than yourself, you seek to help them and encourage them. My friend, you have really learned to love from the heart when you give of yourself as Christ intended. A heart that is caring and concerned for a friend has made a commitment to that person. Isn't that great? If you don't find joy in this idea of concern for others, you may need to examine your life closely.

Jesus Christ has equipped you for certain tasks in life. Have you given thought to your Christian calling? Have you ever considered how you could help someone overcome temptation in their lives? You can help someone overcome any obstacle whenever you feel Christ's call to respond through the Spirit who lives within you. We will discuss this area a little later on in our study.

To summarize our thoughts on temptation in general and the various types of temptations we face, consider the following points:

- Temptation is common to all.
- We all want to overcome it when it enters our lives.
- We need help to defeat temptation.
- Different temptations enter each life.
- Temptation comes from desires, planted like seeds, in our lives. They must either die or grow stronger.
- We often do not need or really want the thing that most tempts us. It may be just the experience itself we seek.
- Christians are indwelt by the Holy Spirit. They should call on the Spirit to help them overcome the things that seek to draw them away from God.
- Christians must select their companions wisely. The Bible has set guidelines for their relationships. Living outside of those guidelines often brings sorrow and division in their lives.
- There is a peace that surpasses understanding in having committed Christians as friends. They can bring joy and peace into our life and lend us their strength as they openly display their love of Christ.

4

Limits of Temptation

Throughout our study we have seen God's hand at work in a variety of areas. We know He cares, for the Bible has said so. I rest in the fact that, as temptation comes, I can resist instead of falling into sin. This is a promise from my loving Father God, and I know He tells the truth.

To the Christian who must fight temptation, know there is a limit to what it is permitted to do to your life. Jesus Christ's death on the cross gave the opportunity to be cleansed of sin daily. When Christ sacrificed His life for us at Calvary, we received a priceless gift from God—foregiveness. All we need to do in order to receive the gift of forgiveness is to ask for it. God looks at us as worthy of forgiveness because Christ died for us. God's Son was very precious to Him. God knows Christ's commitment for our souls. Jesus wanted us to have a personal relationship with Him and to be freed from the yoke of sin. Had Christ not offered His life as an atonement for our sins, we would never have had the opportunity to know God. God hates sin.

Jesus freed us from the evil in our human nature and gave us a precious spiritual nature. All Christians should feel sorrow for wrong attitudes and thoughts. There is no excuse for allowing evil to influence our lives. We must make room for the goodness of the Lord in our hearts. We should repent and ask forgiveness from God because of the sins in our lives. God does not want us to suffer the loss of fellowship because of our sinful nature but desires us to walk in the light with Him. We must want to put aside the old life and take up the new life in Jesus Christ.

CHRISTIANS

God views those who believe and those who refuse to believe in Jesus Christ in a different light. For those who believe and accept Jesus Christ as Lord and Savior of their lives, the way is filled with light. God, you see, is referred to as the light of the world. Satan is referred to as darkness, shadows, ruler of demons, god of this world, and the evil one, among other things. We need to understand the functions of light and darkness in the spiritual realm and what they mean to our lives. Those who believe in Christ stand in the light. Unbelievers are in darkness, spiritual darkness that separates them from the light of the Lord. God looks sadly at sin and will punish those who seek the sinful life.

Everytime I prepare to bring a new and exciting truth to you about Satan and temptation, the attacks come. I want you to understand how important it is to see how Satan seeks to destroy our lives and testimony of faith. For several weeks I have lingered between illness and good health. My blood pressure is high. It has soared like a thermometer on a hot summer day. My sense of balance is distorted. It is difficult to think and reason out the truths of God. I feel very weak and can barely function in my thought processes. The truth about temptation is important. Satan doesn't want you to understand what he is trying to do by corrupting your nature and your spirit. As time goes on, God empowers me to speak the truth to you clearly on the subject. Satan is mad at me, and so the attacks frequently come. Satan hates God, Christ, and those who belong to Christ, in that order. As for the rest of the world, Satan seeks to make them as guilty of rejecting Christ as he is. He torments their lives at his leisure and will continue to do so throughout eternity, if they don't turn to Christ. More about that in the chapter called "Satan: His Character and His Goals." For now, let's look at what temptation can do to those of us who are Christians.

1. Make a list of things you feel Satan is empowered to do through tempting Christians.

a. _____

b. _____

c. _____

d. _____

e. _____

f. _____

2. Now make another list of things you think he cannot do because God draws the line.

a. _____

b. _____

c. _____

d. _____

e. _____

f. _____

Satan can try and test the Christian, but his powers are limited by God. *Always* recall that God is greater than any of Satan's forces. The following verses show us some of the things Satan can do. Write them out in the spaces provided.

I Chronicles 21:1 _____

_____

Job 2:7 _____

_____

Luke 22:31 _____

_____

II Corinthians 11:3 _____

_____

II Corinthians 11:14, 15 _____

_____

Zechariah 3:1 _____

_____

Think of some of the ways you have seen the powers of Satan at work about you. What are some of the sneakiest things that you have seen done in your own community that you believe he had a hand in?

Turn to II Peter 2:9, located before the book of 1 John. *Then the Lord knows how to rescue the godly from temptation, and to keep the unrighteous under punishment for the day of judgment.* Look at what great insight is given us by this one verse.

- God knows how to rescue us from temptation. This must first mean that God knows me. He knows my name, where I live, even what I think. He knows I love Christ. He sees everything that is happening in my life. God isn't dead; He isn't even sleeping. If He knows all about me, surely He is carefully watching and sends answers to my prayers.

- I am a special person to God. My life is not meaningless or haphazard. I am of concern to God. I am more than just one being in the universe; I am a child of God.

- God knows where to draw the line in the areas where I struggle the most. This means that, when the time presents itself, God steps forward and says, "That's enough! No more! Leave my child alone!"

- God has given me the freedom to make choices. Either I will choose to indulge in temptation or I will refuse it. If I say, "yes," God is disappointed. My temptation then becomes a willing act of sin. When I allow sin to rule, I am actually choosing to turn my back on God and do whatever I want at any cost. When I say "no" to temptation and follow God's standards for right and wrong, God is very pleased.

- The unrighteous, the lawbreaker, and the sinner will be punished. God will have each of us stand accountable for willful sin in our lives. That is why we have the freedom to turn our back on sin and temptation. God does not like to punish us, but when we disobey we must be chastened.

Before we said that God is just and able to punish those who hide in the shadows of darkness. Remember the light of God has nothing to do with the darkness of the evil one. Now let's answer the following questions, based on I John 1:5-9.

1. How important is it for the Christian to seek the light that shines from God?

_____

_____

2. What does verse 5 tell you about God and His nature?

_____

_____

3. What is the truth revealed in verse 6 about light (God) and darkness (Satan)? What does this tell you about lies?

_____

_____

4. According to verse 7, what happens when we are in the light with God? What changes do you think we can expect in our character and nature?

_____

_____

5. Whom do we deceive if we say we aren't sinners or have never committed sin in our daily lives? Remember who the liar is? Why would we seek to lie to ourselves when we know the truth about ourselves?

_____

_____

6. What does confession of sin do for us? Why is it necessary for us to seek forgiveness for wrong thoughts, attitudes, and behavior?

_____

_____

7. Temptation, unbridled, leads to sin. What does I John 3:8-10 say about what sin does to our lives?

_____

_____

We noted before that God always gives us a way out, an escape from temptation and trials. It almost seems redundant to repeat that phrase, but we must understand what is happening to us. I think it is vital to understand God's principles of life. We are engaged, Christian and non-Christian alike, in a spiritual war. The enemy will stop at nothing to have his way. He wants to torment and beat us down so badly that we feel no need for God. He wants us to reject Jesus in our life and to be robbed of the happiness found in gaining eternal life through Christ.

Proverbs 1:7 says, *The fear of the Lord is the beginning of knowledge; Fools despise wisdom and instruction.* The instruction of God is to follow right and turn from wrong. Many do not fear God, for they have been deceived into believing He really won't punish us after all. God cannot continue to look upon our willingness to sin with total disregard. He must discipline us for our deliberate disobedience. *For those whom the Lord loves He disciplines, and He scourges every son whom He receives.* (Hebrews 12:6, 7). God chastens those He loves. We should obey and fear the Lord, knowing that He is a just and fair Lord. He will not chastise us without cause. Likewise, He rewards us as He sees fit.

JOB'S TRIAL

And the Lord said to Satan, "From where do you come?" Then Satan answered the Lord and said, "From roaming about on the earth and walking around on it." And the Lord said to Satan, "Have you considered My servant Job? For there is no one like him on the earth, a blameless and upright man, fearing God and turning away from evil." Then Satan answered the Lord, "Does Job fear God for nothing? Hast Thou not made a hedge about him and his house and all that he has, on every side? Thou hast blessed the work of his hand, and his possessions have increased in the land. But put forth Thy hand now and touch all that he has; he will surely curse Thee to Thy face." Then the Lord said to Satan, "Behold, all that he has is in your power, only do not put forth your hand on him." So Satan departed from the presence of the Lord. (Job 1:7-12)

The story of Job is familiar to most of us. Satan was allowed to sift Job to the finest degree as a test of his faith in God. Read this Old Testament story for yourself and learn of Job's dilemma. Job loses everything humanly possible but never curses or turns from God. God allows Satan to try Job almost beyond human measure, but warns, *Spare his life* (Job 2:6). Job was a remarkable man and stood the tests that came his way. He endured severe hardship for his faith.

Job is mocked, reviled, accused, cursed, insulted, and beaten down by Satan's constant attacks. Throughout the entire ordeal, this courageous man never denies God but seeks God's plan of escape. He did as God said he would, he stood firm in faith. Job's example is extremely important for us. He teaches us that we too can overcome the severity of Satan's attacks. God knew Job's heart and the extent of his strength and faith. Bear in mind that God could have called a halt or limited Job's trial at any time, but He did not. God knew how Job would react to his trials, for He knew His servant's heart. God knows your heart and motives too. He wants you to overcome trials and temptations in your life.

UNBELIEVERS

What protection or shield is there for those who have not become Christians? Satan and evil often attack unbelievers and cause them misery and heartache. Their protection from evil is found only in their own powers. They have no spiritual (godly) nature, for the Scriptures tell us God does not acknowledge them.

Turn to the Gospel of John, the fourth book in the New

Testament. Chapter 3, verse 36, reads,⁺*He who believes in the Son has eternal life; but he who does not obey the Son shall not see life, but the wrath of God abides on him.*

Human beings are limited in resources, knowledge, and wisdom in godly matters. We need to fill our lives with the knowledge God has given us through the Scriptures and then use them as weapons in the warfare. The things we learn and appropriate through studying and meditating on God's word will vastly improve our lives. Man is only wise in his own estimation. To God, our wisdom is but folly. Some verses that present this idea are:

- *Has not God made foolish the wisdom of this world?* (I Corinthians 1:20b NKJV).
- *Because the foolishness of God is wiser than men, and the weakness of God is stronger than men* (I Corinthians 1:25 NKJV).
- *For the wisdom of this world is foolishness with God* (I Corinthians 3:19a NKJV).

The unbeliever does not have the power of faith to draw on that the believer in Christ has. They are often caught in the middle of temptation and have no idea what is happening to them. You've seen them, perhaps you've been there—people torn by heartaches and problems with no hope, no way of escape. There seems to be no way out; and life becomes impossible. What has happened to bring this problem on? What can they do? They find no answers in themselves. Desperation and hopelessness set in, and it is difficult to reason through the situation. These moments often make them feel it is impossible to cope. Suicide and death are often considered by persons at this time. Stress is overbearing; life seems hopeless. The desire to end it all is overwhelming. At this moment, they must turn to God in order to receive relief from this problem.

It is sad, but for those who will not look for God or who do not seek to know Him, things won't get better. Their lives and their very souls need God as their main source of strength. Only God can give them a reason to live. Many people turn their backs on God and walk away, again and again, never knowing what life is truly all about. In time, they become hardened and never seek God. They rob their lives of the assurance and peace that God waits to give them. Without God, there is a sense of emptiness and a longing to be filled with *something*. During these moments of hostility, loneliness, and desperation, people often turn to drugs, alcohol, sexual devices, and very often suicide for satisfaction or escape. How sad to shorten one's life and miss the thrill of being a child of God.

There is a brighter side to this for those who really want to escape the torment they are presently living in. When they ask for help and seek guidance from our loving Father through Jesus Christ, they find that Jesus really *is* the answer!

If, perhaps, as you read these words, you need help and want to receive Christ, just pray. How? Allow me to share with you a simple prayer. God will hear if you ask believing and if you truly want to change your life's course. Read it out loud and think of yourself as talking to a living God, for He is alive and cares.

PRAYER "God, I need your help! I don't understand why my life is such a mess and in such turmoil. God, I want to believe You have a better life for me through Your Son, Jesus Christ. I ask You to forgive the sins and wrongs that I have done. Show me a better life by knowing Your thoughts and plans for my life. God, although I know there is a great deal that I don't understand about Jesus, I ask You to show me a new life through Him. Things are such a mess, and I can't find my way without You. I believe Jesus Christ can change my life. I want to live and be happy. Take away the guilt and sadness I feel in my heart. Love me and change me. Thank you, Father, for hearing my prayer. I believe and accept You into my life. Amen."

Great! Now things are going to get better, maybe not all at once, but a little at a time. The next thing you have to do is tell someone what you've done. If you know some Christian people, call them and tell them you have made a decision and accepted Christ into your life. Don't wait! Do it now! If you don't know any people who are Christians, get the telephone book. Turn to the Yellow Pages and locate a church telephone number. Call it. If it is after office hours, look for a minister's home telephone number and call it. If nothing else, call the local police station and tell them you need to talk to a minister or a chaplain. Satan will tell you to wait until tomorrow, but don't do it. Your decision is important to you and to God.

When you get a Christian friend on the telephone, tell him or her what you have done. Tell him or her you haven't been happy with the way life has been going and you want to change. Ask him or her to pray with you or to guide you to someone who will help you understand more. It's going to take determination and a little guts on your part. Remember that God won't let you down. There are a few steps you have to take, but God has an important plan for your life. Begin to look for it today. God loves you. Things will be better for you from now on. Give God time and begin to read the Bible to see what God has said. Turn to the New Testament and begin to read the book of Romans. Romans is the fifth book in the New Testament. Read, study, and pray in your own words.

For the unbeliever, there is a better way—Jesus Christ. There is hope and promise and a reason to be alive. Life need not be hell; it can be much better if you will only believe that Jesus died for your sins and trust God. God loves all of us. John 3:16 says, *For God so loved the world, that He gave His only begotten Son, that whoever believes in Him should not perish, but have eternal life.*

5

The Battle

Before there can be victory in the war against temptation, there must be a battle. There comes a moment when beliefs are put to the test. We believe and trust in Christ as our spiritual Commander-in-Chief. In regular warfare, it is the responsibility of the commander to know the movement of the troops, what weapons, resources, and capabilities are available and to use them at his discretion.

With Christ as the Commander in charge of our life, we need not fear the enemy. The victory will come through our Commander's involvement and through our listening to and following directions. In our battle with temptation, it is our Lord Jesus Christ who has the overall power to engage in the warfare. He shows us how to avoid the pitfalls of life and helps us to overcome. Don't be fooled into thinking this is merely a clever illustration to teach you about temptation and how to deal with it. We are in a serious state of spiritual warfare. Unless we learn to fight the enemy and beat him on his own battle-field, he will overwhelm us.

Before we enter the battle, there are certain preparations we must make. Turn with me to Ephesians 6. Ephesians describes in detail the Christian life and our intended walk with Christ. Let's focus our thoughts on verses 10 through 18.

v. 10:   *Finally, be strong in the Lord, and in the strength of His might.*
   1.   *Be strong in the Lord.* His strength is superior to that of any other.
   2.   *and in the strength of His might.* His might is limitless. It is not bound by time, space, or events of the world.

v. 11:   *Put on the full armor of God, that you may be able to stand firm against the schemes of the devil.*
   1.   When we are completely prepared for the battle, the enemy cannot overpower us.
   2.   The schemes of the evil one are numerous. Without wearing the correct armor of God, and all of it, we will enhance our chances of getting deeply hurt.

v. 12:   *For our struggle is not against flesh and blood, but against the rulers, against the powers, against the world forces of this darkness, against the spiritual forces of wickedness in the heavenly places.*
   1.   We have quite a strong contention of forces standing against us as we enter each spiritual battle. The wise Christian will look at the information available to know the forces they face, so that they can be fully prepared for the conflict that lies ahead.
   2.   Temptation is not the only enemy; rulers, powers, world forces of darkness, and spiritual forces of wickedness can also be enemies.

It looks as though we have our hands full, doesn't it? Well, we do! We must understand there are a variety of different forces that we encounter daily. I expect if we could see these spiritual forces, we would nearly die of fright. This is why the Christian never encounters the enemy alone. If it were not for Christ being on our side, how could we endure? Thus, we must not be unaware of the dangers and of our need to be strong in the faith God has provided for us.

v. 13:   *Therefore, take up the full armor of God, that you may be able to resist in the evil day, and having done everything, to stand firm.*

1.   *Take up the full armor of God.* What is the full armor of God? Where can we get ours? How well will it protect us during the battle? We are about to learn about this special armor. Where do we get it? From God, of course. It is standard equipment for the believer in Christ. God would not have you fight in a battle in which you had no protection. As we will see, God knows the equipment best suited for encountering the enemy on the firing line of life.

2.   *. . . that you may be able to resist in the evil day.* When are the days of evil? That really doesn't seem to need an answer, does it? There are those words again, "that you may be able."

3.   *. . . and having done everything, to stand firm.* When we have been issued the total and complete fighting gear, what remains? The battle. We are to be unwavering in our beliefs and not allow temptation to have its way. Evil often runs a series of bluffs our way before the actual attack occurs. Since we know temptation attacks our weaknesses, we can learn to ignore almost all of the attacks. We need to gain strength through the development of our faith. Only as we clad ourselves in the armor and place our eyes on Christ the Savior can we defeat the enemy. Always recall that we are not to take our eyes from the Christ and glance in the other direction, not for even one short moment.

If we look the other way or glance toward the enemy, a part of our armor slips from place. We become fearful. We are not fully guarded, for we have preoccupied our mind with something else that has caught our view. In fact, we may not even notice that part of the armor God has given us is out of place until the battle begins. This then becomes a dangerous situation, and we are extremely vulnerable at this moment. Remember, eyes on Jesus, our Protector. Before we walk to the front line, we must stop and check to see if our armor is well into place. Then we are ready to begin.

Just what are the pieces of armor God gives us?

v. 14:   *Stand firm therefore, having girded your loins with truth, and having put on the breastplate of righteousness.*

v. 15:   *and having shod your feet with the preparation of the gospel of peace.*

v. 16:   *in addition to all, taking up the shield of faith with which you will be able to extinguish all the flaming missiles of the evil one.*

v. 17:   *And take the helmet of salvation, and the sword of the Spirit, which is the word of God.* It sounds as though God wants us fully dressed in full battle gear, doesn't it? Look at some of the items that make up our battle dress.

1.   *Truth:* What is the important truth in your life? As a Christian, do you maintain a consistent attitude of truth? Bear in mind that temptation lies. God wants us to be truthful and honest in all of our dealings with everyone. Truth does not sway but stands firm at all times.

2.   *Righteousness:* What part should righteousness play in the Christian life? Turn to Romans 3:10 and read it thoroughly. *There is none righteous, not even one.* This is exactly why we need Christ. He sacrificed His life of perfection and truth, so we would be forgiven of our sinful attitudes. We are perfected through Christ. His death was atonement for our sins. He cleansed us. We wear His righteousness as we journey throughout life. This is one reason we should desire a close walk with the Savior.

3.   *Gospel of Peace:* Christ is the Gospel of peace, hope, love, and forgiveness. Were it not for the Gospel of Christ, we would never find contentment and rest in our lives. Christ gives us a reason to live. He turns our sinfulness into forgiveness and peace.

4.   *Shield of Faith:* Our faith in Jesus Christ protects us like an invisible shield. He is the Perfector of our faith. He is our supreme Example of God's love for all people. When we trust and believe in Him, we receive a greater understanding of a life girded by our faith in the Savior, Jesus Christ.

5.   *Helmet of Salvation:* I expect we could spend several days discussing the helmet of salvation. Salvation should not only be a heart-changing experience, it should also be a knowledgeable commitment to Christ. Christ laid His life down for us. In effect, He said, "This person is of value to me. I will give My life for . . . _____ (place your name in each blank), and _____ will be free to experience fullness of life. Because I have given My life as pardon and payment for _____'s sins,

eternal life is available, to _____.

    Grasp the importance of salvation in your life. Christ did not die and leave you and me without hope or a promise. He overcame the powers of evil and arose from the grave. Even the misery of death could not keep Him from joining God the Father. He even told us He would return and claim us for His own. We are free to accept Jesus' gift of salvation and receive the free gift of eternal life because Jesus came and set us free from the yoke of sin.

  6. *Sword of the Spirit:* The Word of God is alive and well. I believe if we were to understand the power of the sword of the Spirit as a tool sent from God, we would use it more often. I assure you, a wise soldier would never enter battle without a weapon. When we know God's Word, we have a powerful weapon at our disposal. Do you know what the Bible teaches us in relation to daily living habits? Pick up your sword and use it. Walk into the battle with confidence, fully prepared to meet the enemy head on. The Lord is with you and His Word is strong.

v. 18: *With all prayer and petition pray at all times in the Spirit, and with this in view, be on the alert with all perseverance and petition for all the saints.* It seems very clear in this stage of the battle that prayers, petitions, and alertness with perseverance are to be our battle instruments. We must pray in the Spirit at all times. If you haven't the Spirit in your life, there isn't much you can do to the enemy. Be sure you are in Christ before you wage a war against evil. Once you are in Christ, know the Holy Spirit has not deserted you as you wage the battle, but He lives within your heart. Draw on the name of the Lord and ask for guidance at all times. The battle will not be waged without notice. There must be a winner and a loser. Remember, you have to want to win, as you wage the war against sin. Pray at all times and step forth in the love of Christ.

THE FURY OF THE BATTLE

Any war is vicious and dangerous. In the spiritual battle in which we are engaged there will be some who are seriously wounded. Still others may be deeply injured, and a few will fall on the field of battle because they did not trust Christ. If we truly want victory in the name of Christ, we will not die on the battlefield. We may receive wounds and engage in some soul-to-soul combat, but we will overcome. No spiritual battle is easy, but the victory is always sweet because it is won through Christ's efforts, not our power.

Bear in mind there is little rest during a battle. You may be called on to fight a lengthy battle. There may be some moments of temptation that are brief, whereas at other times you may fight in an all-out war at length. Each spiritual warfare you encounter may be different. It varies with your spiritual maturity. The enemy is still the same, but his methods vary from temptation to temptation. Remember, it is important how you react. Recalling and following the orders of the Commander-in-Chief will largely determine the outcome of the battle.

Be sure you understand that as confusion comes, it is not from God. God never confuses His people; Satan does. When doubts occur, beware—they are surely not placed there by God. When temptation is at its height, recall that it was never sent from God, for God does not tempt men to do evil. *For God is not the author of confusion but of peace* (I Corinthians 14:33a NKJV).

THOUGHTS DURING THE BATTLE

You may ask, where are my friends when I need them most? You wonder if they have disappeared or perhaps been led astray by the enemy. Perhaps, you think, they just don't care about your problems and needs. Sometimes they seem indifferent when you share your problems with them. Is it that they don't care, or are they just weary of hearing about your problems and trying to help? Don't they know what this battle with temptation is doing to you? They don't seem to understand the needs you have, do they? The questions rumble through your mind, and you are concerned.

Temptation often does some strange things to our minds. We question long-term friendships and motives. Casting doubt is part of the plan to overwhelm your spirit. Doubt often produces anger. It is difficult to understand where your friends have gone when you need them most. If your friends were only here, you think you could overcome the powers of temptation. It may well be that your friends have become preoccupied with their own lives and needs. It is possible that an entirely different temptation has attacked them simultaneously. We forget our friends have their struggles too. We are often so involved with our own needs and problems, we tend to overlook their needs as they do ours. Often we grow angry with friends without reason because we feel they should be more sensitive to us, while all the while they may not even know of our struggle. When they do not react with sensitivity, we become angry. Consider the fact that temptations often draw us in one direction and our friends in another. When this happens, it may be a deliberate attempt to draw both of you away from each other and from God. It may be necessary for you to take the initiative to be with your friends when you need help. We should realize we are not to blame our friends when we get ourselves in a giant mess. You and you alone are responsible for your own reactions to temptation. This stresses the importance of knowing the Word of God and having it planted in your heart to call on as a resource for protection in life. Even when you are without friends or loved ones, there is unlimited strength and knowledge in knowing God's Word and applying these teachings in your heart.

SATAN'S ANGER

Satan really is very angry with us. He wants to pull us away from God anyway he can. He wants to rob you of experiencing the glory of Christ at work in your life. Oftentimes, Christians don't understand this, and when they are tempted they drift away from the Word of God. The further they drift, the more impossible it seems to get back into the Gospel of Christ. Satan has once again bluffed his way through. He has deceived them by making them think there is no way back to God. Many people lose sight of God because they don't call Satan's bluff.

Satan's anger is not necessarily aimed at us. He is angry at God. God has promised to punish Satan for his sins. In the chapter called "Satan: His Character and His Goals," we will take a closer look at him. Satan often strikes back at God through humans, causing temptations to come to them, although he is actually seeking to strike back at God. The Bible says Satan will never give up! He will fight to the bitter end and then fall down at the name of Jesus and worship the Son of God. The story is found in the book of the Revelation. Find a simple version to read of the Bible and read the story for yourself.

Remember, we are to overcome Satan by calling on Christ and by using the Word as our weapon of defense. Always seek to rise above the temptation that surrounds you. Don't allow evil to pollute your mind and heart and impair your vision toward looking to Christ for answers.

6
Dealing with Temptation

So far we have discussed a variety of ideas and thoughts on the subject of temptation. We are now ready to discover how we can conquer the problem. The meat of the issue at hand is how to effectively deal with temptation. Let's get out our spiritual knives and forks and dig into God's Word to see how God instructs us to devour the enemy, temptation.

Christians must learn to walk by obeying God's laws, not Satan's. For too long we have followed Satan's rules and ignored the will of God. As we discover that Satan is, for the most part, running a bluff, we can overcome. To deal with temptation there are certain things we need to know about the nature of temptation:

- Temptation need not be a continual struggle. We can turn it into an opportunity to prove and refine our faith. We can chose new paths to walk instead of the old worn-out path we have walked for a lifetime.

65

- Temptation that recurs has not been properly dealt with. Take a look and see what temptation desires you to do: It seeks to open wide the door of your life, which leads to sin and misconduct.

- Temptation deceives us into believing we are failures and have no other recourse than to surrender and do evil. Temptation seeks to bend and twist our minds out of shape and oftentimes distorts reality. When we lose the reality of God's presence in life, things seem unreal. We become confused and are often misled by various ideas and thoughts. Temptation seeks to give us an alternative to confusion. It says, "You know God doesn't really care. Do anything you want."

- Temptation is a series of lies. These lies are meant to harden your heart's attitude toward God, Christ, other Christians, and the goodness that comes from serving Christ.

- Temptation causes you to examine your life. You must make a decision when temptation occurs and crosses your path. For the Christian, this should be a time to think seriously. What is God trying to help you learn in this adversity and trial? Are you receptive to God's message to you?

- Temptation is knowing that danger may lie ahead. It should be viewed as an effort to distract you from doing right and to lure you into doing wrong. Look at temptation as a bull charging the matador's cape. There is danger and pain ahead if the matador doesn't remove himself from the path of the charger. Common sense says, "Beware of unnecessary danger. Watch carefully as the adversary approaches."

Enough about temptation in your life and the problems it presents. Let's get on with how to deal with the problem. Failure to overcome temptation and adversity causes a serious problem in our lives. Our first step is to have the desire to win in the battle of temptation. You and I must want to feel clean and right before God, not ugly and dirty. We must look to God for His help and ask to be shown the way. We should rejoice, knowing that we can have full fellowship and communion with our Father God. He waits for us to come to Him with our happiness and heartaches and to be glad to live our lives in Him. Turn to God and seek His holy wisdom in every situation you encounter. Wisdom from God is the right understanding of what we should do in life's situations to bring honor to Him.

Turn with me to Romans 12:2 and let's read together. Romans is the sixth book of the New Testament. *And do not be conformed to this world, but be transformed by the renewing of your mind, that you may prove what is that good and acceptable and perfect will of God* (NKJV). God's Word of knowledge is for us not to conform ourselves to the things of the world. Don't give in to wrong. The instruction of the Lord God says to turn away and be transformed by the renewing of your mind. Renew your mind by thinking of the good things God has for you, not the bad. God says that you know in your heart what is right and wrong, so that you are able to choose right.

I challenge your mind and heart to think about the following:

1. God loves me! He has never stopped loving me, not for one instant. He wants the best for me. When changes are necessary, I know He watches my life carefully and gives me options to pursue the best course for my life.

2. For the Christian, the Son of God, Jesus Christ, is the source of strength.

3. God's Son, Jesus Christ, gave my life meaning at the cross of Calvary. Jesus shed His blood as a living sacrifice for me.

4. I, as a Christian, have been adopted by God. When I accepted Christ as Savior and Lord of my life, I received salvation. Salvation is supreme forgiveness by Christ's sacrifice.

5. God supplies my needs according to a plan He has set forth for my life.

6. God wants good in my life so that I might share it with others.

7. God knows my potential. He sees me as a complete person not as having something lacking in my life. He knows me better than I know myself. He has a special task set before me to challenge my Christian life.

8. I believe God and trust Him. He knows what is best for me. I accept this by faith in Christ and will allow God to work in my life. As I do

this, my life opens up and I experience new areas of growth in my Christian maturity.

When I look at my relationship with my Father and consider these truths, I always grow richer in my faith. Knowing God's Word and reading it for myself helps me to overcome the most adverse of circumstances. You and I are <u>often guilty of forgetting what God has said</u>. We become <u>lazy in our study habits</u> and <u>fall into a spiritual rut</u>. It is only as we seek answers that we find them. <u>God works patiently in each life.</u> *thank you Jesus*

1. As you meditate on the eight truths about God we have considered above, which ones have helped you most as you strive to live a Christian life?

   a. _____

   b. _____

   c. _____

   d. _____

2. In which of the points do you need more depth of understanding?

   a. _____

   b. _____

   c. _____

3. Why is it important for us to understand our potential as Christians?

   _____

   _____

   _____

4. What are your long-range goals as a Christian?

_____

_____

_____

5. What is the most important contribution you have ever made as a Christian?

_____

_____

_____

DEALING WITH TEMPTATION

To deal adequately with temptation we will have to look at our lives and make firm decisions. We have learned that temptation will enter our lives regardless of whom we worship. Although Satan tempts Christ's followers consistently, as Christians we should always follow the example set forth by our Savior, Jesus Christ. A careful evaluation of our past should reveal the degree of commitment to Christ as Lord in our lives. Developing a life style pleasing to God and to ourselves takes time, effort, availability, and practice.

1. Ask yourself what kind of life style you seek. Write a summary of your findings below.

_____

_____

_____

_____

2. Second, are you willing to alter your present life style and seek a more godly direction in your life? List those things you are not willing to change. Then ask God to make you willing to have them changed.

_____

_____

_____

3. What do you feel God is trying to tell you about your life?

_____

_____

_____

4. What three areas of temptation and struggle would you most like to have God deal with in your life?

a. _____

b. _____

c. _____

In asking and allowing God to deal with certain areas in your life, you now have given the Lord a place to build on. A better way of life, a happier way through walking with Jesus Christ must begin now. Christ desires you to have peace, happiness, and satisfaction through Him. With choosing to walk with Christ, there will be lasting contentment. Your heart's attitudes will change, and a special joy will continually fill your soul because you chose Christ and have asked Him to work in your heart.

We are to deal with temptation and trials through the knowledge and understanding of the Scriptures. We often neglect our most useful tool—the Word of God—in dealing with life's joys and heartaches. The Bible is God's textbook and guidebook for life. God is a fantastic teacher, relating our situations to examples from real happenings. His commitment to teach His children the importance of obedience and worship is clearly defined in the Bible. Unfortunately, we are not willing to study and learn what God has to teach us. Most of us are lazy and read only bits and pieces of the Bible. We seem to want to read only enough just to get by instead of experiencing the life-changing results that come through the study of His Word.

I think God would remind us, like any good teacher, that there are going to be tests and even a final exam. Each of us will have to stand before Him and watch as He examines our lives. What will He see when He reviews our lives? I fear we will all wish we had studied and learned more from God's Word and had been much better than we really were. God wants us to be adequately informed about the course He has set for our lives. We should always approach studying the Scriptures as an opportunity to know God better and to learn from Him.

There are several keys to overcome temptation. Let's concentrate on them for a few moments.

GIVE YOUR LIFE
TO THE LIVING LORD

Let's examine some of the passages that encourage us in this area.

1. Romans 12:21 reads, *Do not be overcome by evil, but overcome evil with good* (NKJV). We cannot overcome evil on our own. The overall power is not within us. Only Jesus Christ is good and perfect. He was sinless and never yielded, and He stands as our Defender.

2. Trust the Lord. Romans 8:26-28 reads, *Likewise the Spirit also helps in our weakness. For we do not know what we should pray for as we ought, but the Spirit Himself makes intercession for us with groanings which cannot be uttered. Now He who*

searches the hearts knows what the mind of the Spirit is, because He makes intercession for the saints according to the will of God. And we know that all things work together for good to those who love God, to those who are called according to His purpose (NKJV).

When we look at these verses we should be thrilled and excited. What more could we want? We have the Spirit living within us as a part of our life. The Holy Spirit changes our entire attitude and capacity to love. When I first realized the implication of this, I became overjoyed. For the Spirit to indwell me, I must be pretty special. Soon I learned that God refers to us as His adopted children. This important truth affirmed the idea that I was special, and so are you if you have Christ. Friends, if that idea doesn't bring joy and happiness to your heart, you may need to see a doctor. You may just be dead or pretty close to it. Christ brings meaning to life.

The Spirit Himself makes intercession for us. . . . Think about that for a minute. The Holy Spirit considers your needs and then goes to God the Father. There's a One-to-One conversation, God the Father and God the Holy Spirit. He explains our situation and asks, on your behalf, for an answer. Do you see how important you are? The things you cannot deal with in your own intelligence, wisdom and power are given over to the Supreme Might and Power, God.

Our Intercessor makes our petition known to God the Father and seeks God's will in the matter. God's will is always what is best for us. Do you realize how important it is for us to look for God's will and not our own? We think we know what is best in our lives and often make some terrible blunders. *God* knows what is best and never makes an error in judgment.

And we know that all things work together for good to those who love God (Romans 8:28 NKJV). We know what? That *all* things work together for good? I can almost hear you say, "Surely, not *all* things!" Yes, friends, *all* things work together, like putting together all the pieces in a puzzle. He together, like putting together all the pieces in a puzzle. He knows where the pieces fit together to make the picture complete. He sees the master plan and views our lives in a far different perspective than you or I. God knows what is good for our lives. He can help us achieve the proper goals.

The reason we struggle so desperately with problems is due in part to our desire to avoid God. We rebel and fight because we desire to do "our own thing." The Christian who finally comes to grips with this situation can receive help. God helps us by enlarging our capacity to overcome temptation. We don't have to struggle with our inadequacies; we don't have to be our own worse enemy. When we really understand God, we are free to experience life in all its fullness. God meets you where you are. He helps you to mature spiritually and blesses you according to your understanding of the Word and your willingness to follow His will.

Remember, the first rule in dealing with temptation is to trust Christ. He really does know what is best for you. Consider those times from the past when you knew Christ helped you. Christ shed light and glory on your Christian life. Christ imparted understanding and wisdom in your situation, and He will do the same for you now. Satan, on the other hand, leads you into darkness and shadows and fills you with unhappiness, grief, and sin. Satan wants to frustrate and confuse your life and make you inoperable. Friends, this is true! It's time for us to face up to our situation. We will never on our own overcome the powers that seek to overcome and weaken us. Jesus is the answer. Only Jesus can give us understanding and love.

RESIST TEMPTATION
AND THE DEVIL

There is a Scripture in the book of James, chapter 4, verse 7, that says, *Submit therefore to God. Resist the devil and he will flee from you.* There are two important facts in this verse for us to understand.

First, we are to submit our minds and hearts to the call of the Lord God. Give Him our all and then place ourselves in His hands, knowing we are secure in our faith and trust. Second, resist the devil. Don't let him have his way! Fight the battle and rebuke what he is seeking to do to you. Temptation wants you to believe you have no other recourse than to submit to it. Nothing could be more foolish than to accept this hideous suggestion.

Verse 10 gives a clear view of what must follow submission to God. *Humble yourselves in the presence of the Lord, and He will exalt you.* Until we learn the value of a humble heart, we will never experience the fullness of the Spirit. We need not be proud of who we are in ourselves, but of who we are because of Christ. When we humble our spirits, we receive a capacity to understand and experience Christ anew.

REBUKE IN THE NAME OF THE LORD

But Michael the archangel, when he disputed with the devil and argued about the body of Moses, did not dare pronounce against him a railing judgment, but said, "The Lord rebuke you" (Jude 9). We cannot send evil from our lives without the power of the Lord. Even the archangel Michael, with his might and powers, knew where to draw the line in dealing with the Devil. Always remember the Devil cannot overcome the Lord Jesus Christ. He could not defeat Christ at the cross by setting the circumstances for His death. Christ overcame death. There is no power superior to that of Christ's!

A fair warning for Christians who feel, because they have faith and belief in Christ, that they can outmaneuver the Devil. Don't think that you can play games with the Devil and set him up in a series of tests; you can't. You may well fall victim to one of his schemes and plans. Overconfidence in self instead of in Christ will cause you many heartaches. Spiritual warfare is no game. There are Christians who, having experienced the power of Christ in their lives, seek to maneuver the powers of light and darkness against each other.

When we rebuke the Devil in the name of Christ and know we have done so with a genuine spirit of faith and belief, Satan must go away. He knows that the Lord will not tolerate his foolishness and that he must go. He will seek to return at a more opportune time, but for now he must walk away from the battle.

We are never to look for a particular encounter with the Devil, for it only leads to additional heartaches and problems. Instead of spending our time rebuking him, we are to avoid him and his evil altogether. If we will take the effort to ignore temptation when it comes, we will keep ourselves from overexposure to evil. Even Jesus ignored Satan and finally rebuked him using Scriptures.

In some areas of our lives, it is far better to walk away from the enemy than to have an old-fashioned brawl. We aren't to have our noses bloodied by evil, but we are to resist evil and avoid the blows of the attacker. The battle is far more serious than you and I can handle without Christ as our Defender. Remember, that as we are forced into battle, we must be clad in the full armor of God as found in Ephesians 6.

SET YOUR MIND
ON THE THINGS ABOVE

When you are alone and daydreaming, what comes to your mind? What occupies your mind as you sit in the airport waiting for your flight to arrive from another city? Do you consider things that set your mind and nerves afire? Are you pulled into the realm of considering what might be fun or satisfying when given an opportunity for a brief chance? Perhaps you have a strong compulsion to have a relaxing drink. One drink will help ease the tension and strain of the day; two will make you feel looser; three will have your mind roving in search of some adventure. Strange things happen when we are alone with loneliness and emptiness that come from separation from those we love. Temptation knows how to sneak in and cause our weaknesses to pull us toward a quest for excitement and happiness, even for just a few moments at a time.

Temptation conceals lust under the subtle guise of harmless flirtation. There seems to be a constant lure of temptation to satisfy self, especially for those who travel. My husband, a consultant, travels a great deal. His job takes him to many airports, and he is faced with various kinds of temptations. He often relates how difficult traveling is on a married man. Temptation presents itself everywhere people go. Seeing temptation on a larger scale than I, he says, "You just wouldn't believe some of the things that I see. The world seems to be going crazy." I don't ask any questions. I figured out some time back that I was too naive about some of the things he tells me anyway. I am basically very trusting and don't see many areas that lead to dangerous traps. He says that he has learned the value of neither looking right nor left but of walking straight ahead and that when we take our eyes off of Christ, the temptations multiply. The Scriptures say this is a wise thing to do, to set our mind on Christ. For those who in difficult situations with many temptations, I feel sure that God has a plan to help you too. Remember, think on the things of God.

Turn with me to the third chapter of Colossians and begin to read verse 2, *Set your mind on the things above, not on the things that are on earth.* What a beautiful idea!

This beautiful verse gives us an important piece of information. Let's view it in all its splendor:

- I need to set my mind on Christ. Before I can set my mind on Christ, I must clear all unnecessary thoughts out of my mind. Forget about supper, the kids, football games, progress reports, anything that would distract me from Christ, as nothing else but Jesus should be seen in my mind's eye.

- Seek to <u>think godly thoughts</u>. Know that God is present in the spirit and seek to understand the things He seeks to teach my spirit that I might gain Christian maturity. As I consider His might and power, I gain in spiritual wisdom and knowledge.

- <u>Don't think of the things</u> that are on the earth while dwelling on Christ. Almost every other thing distracts my attention from Christ. Don't look around and be <u>led astray by a variety of thoughts</u> and <u>ideas. The world around us seeks to draw us away from the ministry Christ has for us</u>. When we dwell on other thoughts, there is not room for Christ. We simply cannot fit Him in. Temptation distracts us.

You know, I always seem to think about something other than Christ. Have you experienced the same attitude in your life?

Women often dress to draw men's attention to them. Just this morning I watched a woman in a black, low-cut blouse enter the post office. Men were unconsciously reacting to what they saw. No doubt this woman thought she looked quite sexy; the men thought so too. In my mind's eye, I thought there was absolutely no need for her to have the first three buttons of her silk blouse undone.

She knew what she wanted and no doubt before this day was over, she wound up having it. Her walk, dress, and mannerisms left no doubt that she sought to lure the attention of the opposite sex. I say this not to be a prude, or old fashioned, but honestly, ladies, we should learn to use discretion in our dress as well as in our thoughts.

EYES ON JESUS

Therefore, since we have so great a cloud of witnesses surrounding us, let us also lay aside every encumbrance, and the sin which so easily entangles us, and let us run with endurance the race that is set before us, fixing our eyes on Jesus, the author and perfecter of faith, who for the joy set before Him endured the cross, despising the shame, and has sat down at the right hand of the throne of God (Hebrews 12:1, 2). There it is! The number-one answer to our need—keep our eyes on Jesus.

Why are we to place our center of attention on Jesus?

1. He is the Perfecter of our faith.
2. He is our invincible Soldier who overcomes evil through our gift of salvation.
3. He endured shame at the cross, so that we might not have to surrender to sin.
4. He cares for us. When all else fails, Christ remains the same. (Hebrews 13:8 says, *Jesus Christ is the same yesterday and today, yes and forever.*) What a comfort to realize that Christ will not waver or change direction. He provides us with steadfastness and security for all our days.

At this point in our study, let us ask ourselves a few questions.

1. How can God allow temptation to make me a stronger Christian?

_____

_____

_____

_____

2. What is the function of temptation for improving my spiritual condition? How can it improve my walk with Christ? (Read Deuteronomy 8:2.)

_____

_____

_____

_____

The Bible relates the idea that temptation is a method of examining our heart. When temptation comes, do we keep the commandments? It always exposes evil, wrong attitudes, wickedness, ungodliness, and spiritual pride in our lives. Temptation displays our open rebelliousness against God and the dark areas of our lives that need attention and changing. Very often we feel we have not yet "arrived" in our Christian lives. Spiritual growth comes painfully slow.

Those who seek a close relationship with the living Lord gain some startling revelations during prolonged periods of temptation. Temptation teaches us that we still have some distance to travel in reaching perfection in our lives. The wise Christian can use the struggle with temptation as an opportunity for growth. When we refuse the call of temptation and forbid it to have its way, we become more receptive to the Spirit of the Lord. Spiritual growth is a daily process and is not gained in one large measure. It takes time, patience, suffering, and endurance to grow. It has been my experience that each time I think I have "arrived" or am gaining ground, I have not! Each of us has areas that need some improvement.

None of us will ever know perfection in our lives as Christ knew it. Not matter how close we feel we may be to our loving Lord, we are often still further away than we realize. Although He blesses us with spiritual encouragement and abundantly shares His riches with us, if we reach the point when we think of ourselves as being superior or more knowledgeable than any other person, then we have fallen into a snare of pride. This attitude is disturbing to the Lord as well as to other Christians. Regardless of how we view our gifts and talents, God views none as more valuable than the other. There is no room for spiritual pride and puffed-up egos in the circle of those who share faith in Christ. We can never be mature Christians as long as we cling to our spiritual egos and superficial pride. We are not to be ignorant that Satan will use these to bring us down. In II Corinthians 2:11b it states that *we are not ignorant of his devices.*

ENCOURAGERS

Christians who keep their eyes on Jesus have many great blessings in store for them. When tempted, think about Christ and His concern for you. I will share a list of Scriptures with you for you to begin your meditations. In Sunday school I designated a special title when sharing these Scriptures: encouragers. Encouragers strengthen your heart and help you concentrate on Jesus. They are an invaluable tool. You might like to carry a copy of these verses along with you each day. Read them for those moments that seem impossible to bear. Make your own list of Scriptures that can be your own special source of encouragement.

1. *These things I have spoken to you, that in Me you may have peace. In the world you have tribulation, but take courage; I have overcome the world* (John 16:33).

2. *For the wages of sin is death, but the gift of God is eternal life in Christ Jesus our Lord* (Romans 6:23 NKJV).

3. *God is faithful, through whom you were called into fellowship with His Son, Jesus Christ our Lord* (I Corinthians 1:9).

4. *No temptation has overtaken you but such as is common to man; and God is faithful, who will not allow you to be tempted beyond what you are able, but with the temptation will provide the way of escape also, that you may be able to endure it* (I Corinthians 10:13).

5. *God is not a God of confusion but of peace...* (I Corinthians 14:33).

6. *Brethren, rejoice, be made complete, be comforted, be like-minded, live in peace; and the God of love and peace shall be with you* (II Corinthians 13:11).

7. *Stand fast therefore in the liberty by which Christ has made us free, and do not be entangled again with a yoke of bondage* (Galatians 5:1 NKJV).

8. *And let us not grow weary while doing good, for in due season we shall reap if we do not lose heart* (Galatians 6:9 NKJV).

9. *Whatever good anyone does, he will receive the same from the Lord, whether he is a slave or free* (Ephesians 6:8 NKJV).

10. *My brethren, count it all joy when you fall into various trials, knowing that the testing of your faith produces patience. But let patience have its perfect work, that you may be perfect and complete, lacking in nothing* (James 1:2-4 NKJV).

11. *There is no fear in love; but perfect love casts out fear, because fear involves torment. But he who fears has not been made perfect in love. We love Him because He first loved us* (I John 4:18, 19 NKJV).

12. *Be anxious for nothing, but in everything by prayer and supplication with thanksgiving let your requests be made known to God* (Philippians 4:6).

As you can see, these encouragers are a source of strength and enlightenment. They are vitamins for the soul. By reading the Words of God there is help. We can begin to see God in a different light. Our task is to ground our lives in the knowledge of what God has said on certain subjects. We will discuss this idea in depth in a few minutes.

When we begin to study the Scriptures verse by verse, I really get excited. Anyone in my Sunday school class would vouch for this. As I compile the list of passages for class, I usually get caught up in my task and end up with a list several pages long. What happens is this: As I prepare to teach and share, I set my total concentration on Christ. As I read the Scripture truths that apply to the lesson, my soul soars. I love to share the Scriptures this way. I urge you to give this method a try. Focus your undivided attention on Jesus Christ, not only as your Lord and Savior, but as your Teacher, Helper, and Best Friend.

STOP, LOOK,
AND LISTEN TO GOD

When I was a girl in Memphis, Tennessee, I recall a lesson at school on warning signals and the presence of danger in our lives. The purpose was to teach us to observe warning signs at railroad crossings by these rules: Stop, look, and listen. There weren't many electric signals to warn of approaching trains, so we depended on our senses. I remember a song that reminded us to stop, look both ways, and listen for sounds that were out of the ordinary. God has provided us with some warning signs of danger in our spiritual lives. To know them we must read the Bible. It is our major resource material for life. Contained in its pages is the inspired Word of God. We should become familiar with its teachings and apply them to our hearts and lives.

So, then, the Holy Bible is one of our major tools in building a strong faith. Consider how much God loves us by giving us the Bible. He did not leave us to wander around in the deserts of life without a clearly defined map to lead us to the oasis of life. The Scriptures contain numerous answers to some of life's most perplexing problems. But before the Bible can be practical and meaningful, it is necessary for us to read it. The only real way to know what the Bible has to say to us is to read it for ourselves.

Perhaps we are relying on others to read the Word of God and pass along their interpretation to us. Frankly, most of us seem just a bit lazy, perhaps preoccupied is a better word, and just don't take the time to read the Bible as we should. What a strange situation we find our spiritual lives in because we are depending on someone else to lend us their understanding of the Scriptures to carry us through our spiritual lives. I wonder if we understand the impact this has on our lives? We would never allow just anyone to make the final decision for us in dealing with our financial matters or in deciding how we should spend our lives. Likewise, we wouldn't want someone to paint our home or install solar heating without our complete consideration of the matter and all of the factors involved. Why, then, do we depend entirely on others to give us their understanding of what God's Word has said? God may have an entirely different truth to reveal to us as we read the Bible.

We must examine our lives to determine the real reasons

we do not read and study the Bible to find answers to the problems we face in our daily living.

- We are spirtitually immature. We do not read because we do not strive to grow and mature as Christians. Somehow we have convinced ourselves that there are more important things to do. Sitting down and reading the Bible takes away time that might be spent doing other things.
- Unfortunately, most of us are a bit lazy at times. We would rather spend the time taking a nap or doing something that we consider much more fun. Let someone else read the Bible. If there is something important to know, someone will be more than willing to share it with us.
- We can be, at least, partially blinded to our spiritual senses and feelings. II Peter 1:9, John 1:6; 2:4, 9, 11, and numerous other verses point to the truth in this matter. Temptation yielded to results in sin, which breaks our fellowship with the Father. As this occurs, we are susceptible to spiritual blindness. Spiritual blindness is a fascinating area of study. When you have the time and the opportunity, dig into the subject and learn more about it. Spiritual blindness and deafness are often caused by our lack of sensitivity to the Holy Spirit speaking within us.
- In our minds we reason that knowing what the Bible has to say really isn't all that important. "I'll begin tomorrow to read and study," seems to be another way of putting it off. The largest problem is that tomorrow never comes! We put off Bible reading and promise ourselves, "Tomorrow for sure!" We always seem to be busy and just don't have enough time to do the things we really want to do.

We must find a way to break out of the trap of indifference. It is difficult to learn the truths of the Scriptures when we really have no idea what they are. You see, our Bible was written by our Master Teacher, God. Each of us is free to experience the truth of God's plan for ourselves. When we read a passage, it might well change our lives and alter the course we are presently traveling.

Depending on what God has to teach you and the work He

has stored up for you to do, you learn from God at your own pace. Each of us is on a different spiritual level, and God treats us as individual persons. We can gain considerable wisdom and insight as we study God's textbooks of life—the Bible. He is so very good to us and teaches each of us at a level of understanding that helps us to grow and mature.

Friends of mine who are teachers tell me that teaching one to one is the most effective method of teaching. In their classroom situations, it is very often impossible to share with a student in this manner. While they would delight in teaching each student one to one, their time is limited. Not so with God! He has the time and the patience to teach us on an individual basis. We need only be eager to learn and desire God to teach us.

God is the most brilliant of teachers. He never gets tired of showing us His truths. His lesson plans never need updating or renewal. His teachings are timeless and never outdated. God is infinite in wisdom and knowledge and desires to share these things with those who love Him.

PRAYER

The next step in overcoming the powers of temptation is prayer. Prayer is an important tool and is most effective when we are in some of the situations which seem to overwhelm us. I believe it would thrill your mind and make your spirit soar to share in a time of prayer with God each day of your life. When we pray with an earnest heart and in the belief that God hears and answers prayer, we will see results in our lives.

We should never underestimate the power of prayer in our lives. As we take the opportunity to pray and allow the Holy Spirit to speak within us, things will begin to happen. I can almost guarantee that as you approach the Lord with a humble spirit and in brokenness of spirit, He will hear you. You will receive an answer to your prayer, although you may have to wait for God's timing and His will to be revealed. Remember, there may be a short delay in receiving an answer, for not all prayers are answered without the passing of some time.

Very often we want to push God into answering our prayers ahead of His timetable. The results may not be what we expect or He may even answer "no." But God will answer in time. It may take a while for us to change some of our attitudes or God may wait for certain other situations to be altered before your prayer is answered, but God does answer. God never works in a haphazard manner to achieve the perfect results He has in mind. Remember that in waiting our faith is made stronger. We learn to wait patiently, knowing He has everything under control.

There are times when God doesn't make us wait for prolonged periods of time. God knows each person's request and never makes mistakes. Sometimes we tend to pressure God and call for immediate answers. We are always in a hurry to get what we want and sometimes just don't want to wait on God's answer. This can lead us to making decisions, thinking we know what God wants us to do, when He has not given us the answer yet.

Some answers are immediate, according to the need. None of us can judge when God will answer a prayer immediately and when we must wait for the results of God's answer. God knows how to judge our prayer requests in a supreme manner that is not understood by man and woman. We must simply accept and trust what God does in our lives.

In a situation where temptation is involved, we often feel God cannot answer too quickly to suit us. Always remember to pray when you need to. No matter where you are or what the need is, God is concerned for you! Ask God to supply you with a way of escape when you are tempted, one you can clearly see and understand. Ask if there is an answer before you that will help you sidestep the situation you are presently faced with. God doesn't get weary of your prayers and your seeking for His direction. Give thanks and know He has heard your prayer. As a Christian, you have the power, through Christ the Lord, to overcome any circumstances that enter your life. Not even temptation need overpower the Spirit that lives within you.

The next step is to remove yourself and get away from the thing that is tempting you. Only a fool would stand and think the temptation would diminish without some effort. Flee, move out of the area that seeks to engulf you. There is potential evil and sin lurking about you. Remember, you are in a situation that presents numerous problems and possible heartaches in your life. Get away from it, don't look back at it, turn aside, and think of a place of safety.

To remove yourself from the path of temptation takes strong willpower. You have that willpower through Christ the Lord. As you flee, begin to pray. I can almost hear you say, "What should I pray about?"

Well, I do have an answer for you, pray for any situation other than the one you're in, one in which you know there is a need.

1. Pray for your wife, husband, children, parents, teachers, just about anyone you know who needs prayer.

2. Pray for your friends. "Dear Lord, I want to pray for my friend _____. You know how my friend struggles and needs your help in the area of _____."

Talk to the Lord about your friends. Pray for them from your heart. Ask the Lord exactly how you should pray for them. Pray that the Lord would reveal to you the needs your friends have, and ask that you might understand some new truth about your friend so that you might be a better friend to them.

Do you see the importance in this manner of prayer? You have taken your eyes from your need, and now you are looking to the needs of another. I can assure you that your friends and neighbors need prayer and many secretly wish someone would pray for them.

3. Pray for your church, your pastor, or someone in the congregation.

4. Pray for those who share the love of Christ with you. All Christian denominations need to be lifted up in prayer.

One of the reasons we are tempted so often is because we tend to concentrate on ourselves. Friends, I have got some news for you. The Bible tells us we should consider other people as more important than ourselves. When we grasp this truth and apply it to our lives, something fantastic will happen. The Spirit will show us how we can serve others in a manner worthy of Jesus. By looking at all others as more important, not just our little circle of friends, we understand the concept of loving as Christ loved—impartiality. This kind of concern results in unselfish giving as we focus our attentions on sharing of ourselves in genuine Christian love. Each of us should learn to generously give love from the heart and to freely share our faith in Christ. Isn't that great? Only as we grasp this idea and serve with the love of Christ can true happiness be found in our hearts. Christianity is the genuine giving and sharing of Christ in us with all persons.

I could write a book on the idea of loving one another as Christ truly intended us to. I honestly believe we have become so involved in our own lives that we have almost entirely missed the concept of loving one another in Christlike love. Why don't you pray for others from deep within your heart and watch how your life will be enriched? Give it a try and experience some heart-warming results.

Once you have finished praying for Mary, pray for someone else. Pray for your church, your minister, the churches in your area. Temptation strikes in all areas of life. There is a need for God to work among all who are followers of Christ. Don't you think it is time for us to cross over denominational lines and just love one another as Christians? Christ knows us, not by denominations, but by our names and personalities. Remember, we are all precious to Him. Pray for those in the faith as we are taught to in the Scriptures:

- I Thessalonians 5:25: *Brethren, pray for us* (NKJV).
- Hebrews 13:18: *Pray for us* (NKJV).
- Colossians 4:12: *Epaphras, who is one of your number, a bondslave of Jesus Christ, sends you his greetings, always laboring earnestly for you in his prayers, that you may stand perfect and fully assured in all the will of God.*

As you pray, temptation begins to lose some of its interest in you. You see, you have focused your attention elsewhere. It is more difficult to get your attention now, and very quickly temptation will leave you. It will then go and bother someone else who isn't praying but who is more receptive to the idea of temptation. Prayer is very valuable in your life and mine. I hope you have begun to use it wisely on a daily basis and understand its importance.

CHRISTIAN MEDITATION

Each time I hear the word *meditation* my mind drifts to some far-off land. There is a little old man with a white beard sitting on the floor. I expect you've seen one like him on television or in a film. His body is wrapped around him much like a pretzel. I often think that I wish I could do that and still get up when I was finished. My body says, "Don't try it, you'll never make it." My mind drifts still a bit further as I watch this man who appears to be in a trance. Someone is poking needles and all kinds of hideous things in his skin. Since this fellow is in a deep trance, he doesn't feel the pain. It looks hideous and painful. Friends, for the Christian this is not meditation. We can meditate on Christ at any time, anywhere. We need no special items to inflict pain and suffering to prove our faith. We need only to prepare our heart and spirit and seek to receive a lesson from Him. You only need to be quiet and think of Christ. Listen and allow Him to speak to your heart.

What happens when we give Christ our uninterrupted time and attention? We feel His presence in our souls! That's a very wonderful experience. *Let my meditation be pleasing to Him; As for me, I shall be glad in the Lord* (Psalm 104:34). Glad is a very simple expression of happiness. You will be glad as temptation comes and you begin to meditate and think of Jesus Christ. When you truly concentrate on what Christ has done in your life, what He is doing, and what He could possibly do for you, there should be an abundance of gladness and a sense of overwhelming love and appreciation within your soul. Christians, know that Christ is concerned and that He knows you personally!

There is so very much more to the Christian life than most of us have discovered. We almost seem afraid to let Christ work in our lives, and therefore we miss many blessings. When you are tempted, think, "Just what is it that Christ has for me to do? How am I to deal with this situation and overcome it? What am I to learn or change from this experience? Christ, what would You have me to be in order that I might experience Your love to the utmost? What goals have You set before me? Make a list of answers to each of these questions and be thankful you believe in Him.

Think Jesus Christ! It really isn't all that difficult. Try it! The Holy Spirit within you desires to reveal a life filled with joy, peace, and happiness to you. Christian, do you really understand that the Holy Spirit lives inside you and is a part of your daily life? When you need to find a reason to be glad about something, meditate on that for a while. Satan would have you feel you are nothing; don't you believe that lie for one minute! You are a precious child of the living Lord.

As you pray, think of what you would like to do with your life. Have you ever asked Christ how you can best serve Him? Is there some task He has set aside for you? Think about your personal relationship with the living Lord, and allow Him to be a vital part of your life. To be an instrument used for Christ's work is truly an exciting experience.

The first time I heard this idea a friend of mine, Jane Rachel, and I were sitting under a shade tree in her back yard. Although Jane and I belong to different denominations, we still share the agape love of Christ and are special friends. We have often talked about Christ and shared ideas with each other. Jane has been a great comfort to me as I have matured as a Christian throughout the years. I am thankful for a friend like Jane, who has the courage to share her faith with her friends. Although some of our views may be different, we both love Christ and each other. At some points in my life I could scarcely endure as I grew in faith. Jane has given me strength and courage to walk on. Her faith is sure and positive as she shares it with me. One day when we were talking, she said, "Frances, have you claimed all Christ has for you? Have you really asked Him what He had for you to do?"

Jane's words pulled at my heart and took root. I thought for a moment and replied, "No, I don't guess that I have." The more I considered the idea, I knew I hadn't. "Jane, I don't know how to find His will and purpose for my life. What do I have to do? How do I know? How can I learn?"

Instead of giving me a pat answer or some cute cliché, she answered this way, "Let me tell you something my mother once told me. Frances, mother had always been a good Christian woman and walked with Christ, but she knew something was missing in her life. Mother began to pray about it. She asked Christ to reveal to her whatever He had for her. She told Him she was willing to make any changes and do whatever it took. She said that her life began to change almost immediately. That's how mother found what Christ had for her, she asked and then accepted His gifts."

I meditated on my friend's words for some while. "You mean that all I have to do is ask and it will happen?" I asked. She smiled and nodded her head. I had struggled for months with my life, seeking a sense of direction and purpose. I had become restless and unhappy as I grew, knowing there was more to the Christian life than I presently understood. I felt there was something special for me, but I just couldn't find it. I desperately wanted to be Christ's person all the time. I longed to serve Him. I meditated about my conversation with Jane that afternoon until late that night. I wasn't sure I was willing to make such a commitment. Would I be willing to give up my life and anything that was unpleasing to God? How could I possibly live a life giving up things I wanted? I struggled all night with these questions.

The next morning I called Jane. When she answered the phone, I began to question her again on the subject. I am thankful to have such a patient and loving friend who is strong in her faith. I asked, "Jane, how can I possibly do anything that Christ asks me to do? How can I follow through? How can I change my life and do whatever Christ says? I really want to do this thing and do whatever Christ wants me to do, but I'm not that strong. Jane, I am really struggling with this problem."

"Frances, you don't have to rely on your own strength and power but on His. Christ will show you the way and open the doors. Remember, He never gives us more than we can handle. You will know when you must make this commitment. There will be no doubt at all in your mind and heart," she said with complete confidence.

I struggled for a long while about total surrender of my life and attitudes to Christ. I wanted to make a full commitment, yet I was hesitant. Finally in despair and brokenness of my old spirit I began to pray once again. As I thought about Christ I saw Him in a different light. Christ did not hold back on His task while He was on earth. Had Christ said "no" to God, our lives would have been completely hopeless. We would never have experienced one moment of peace or happiness. I prayed and wept for a very long while. Then I spoke, "Lord, I really do want to be the kind of person You want me to be. I want to do anything You have for me to do. Lord, show me how and what to do, so my life can be filled and complete. I'm Yours, Lord! Amen."

The more I thought about Christ and my life, the happier I became. It seemed as though a great burden was lifted from my heart. I knew life would be different now. I saw Christ standing before me, "I gave My all for you, Frances. I want you to follow after Me and serve Me with all of your heart, soul, and mind for all the days of your life. I will show you the way. I have something special waiting for you. I will teach you all you need to know and will open many doors for you. Be faithful and trust in Me. I will not let you down but will bless your life abundantly when you do what I command of you."

My life did change, and the opportunities to serve Christ have been numerous. When Christ opened the door of opportunity to write, I was baffled. I asked, "Lord, are You sure this is the thing You want me to do?" And as if I had to remind Him, "Lord, I'm forty years old and have never written a word in my life." His answer, "You promised you would do whatever I asked. Do it gladly! I will teach you and open up your life to a new area of service. I have work for you to do and the opportunities will freely flow as you remain faithful to your promise." What more could a Christian ask than to be used by Christ? I am blessed!

Meditate on the Lord whenever possible. Don't allow yourself to be so involved with other things that you miss the joy of the presence of the Savior in your life. As a source of encouragement, look up these Scriptures and write them in the blanks provided for you below.

Psalm 19:14 _____

_____

_____

Psalm 49:3 _____

_____

_____

Psalm 119:11, 15, 16 _____

_____

_____

_____

I Timothy 4:14, 15 _____

_____

_____

_____

Do you have a private time of meditation with Christ?
What are the benefits or rewards of having a time of thinking about Christ only?

_____

_____

_____

_____

_____

_____

_____

THANKSGIVING

In everything give thanks; for this is God's will for you in Christ Jesus (I Thessalonians 5:18). Why? Turn to Romans 8:28. Romans is located, as you will recall, after the book of Acts and before the book of Galatians. Write out your findings below:

_____

_____

When temptation comes we must begin with the correct approach and a positive attitude. We must say to ourselves, "This temptation does not have to defeat me or bother me. I give thanks that Christ knows my heart. I have the heart of Christ, and I can give thanks that He trusts me. Christ lives in me because I have received the gift of salvation through Him. What can separate me from the love of Christ?" Read Romans 8:35, 36 for yourself, and list the seven situations mentioned that cannot separate you from Christ's love.

1. _____

2. _____

3. _____

4. _____

5. _____

6. _____

7. _____

Now look at verse 37 and note this marvelous truth: *But in all these things we overwhelmingly conquer through Him who loved us.* Isn't that exciting? Temptation hasn't a leg to stand on. Christ is the answer, and temptation cannot hide that truth from your heart.

We should really be thrilled as we understand that giving thanks in all things is telling Christ we really do know He cares for us.

REJOICING

Aren't rejoicing and giving thanks almost the same thing? you might ask. No, not really. You rejoice when you overcome temptation, for you know you have endured and stood the attack of the evil one. The Christian life is meant to be a good experience, not a miserable one. Christians, we need to rejoice and be happy for we have found peace of mind and heart through our Savior Christ. *Let your forbearing spirit be known to all men. The Lord is near. Be anxious for nothing, but in everything by prayer and supplication with thanksgiving let your requests be made known to God. And the peace of God, which surpasses all comprehension, shall guard your hearts and your minds in Christ Jesus* (Philippians 4:5-7).

Rejoice in the Lord always; again I will say, rejoice! (Philippians 4:4). How often does Paul tell us we should rejoice because we can overcome anything, even the most adverse circumstances? Paul makes it clear—always!

Paul advises us to let our minds dwell on certain things. Turn to Philippians 4:8 and read this important set of instructions for our lives. Use the spaces provided to make a complete list of the things that Paul considers important for us to dwell on.

a. *whatever is* _____

b. *whatever is* _____

   c. *whatever is* _____

   d. *whatever is* _____

   e. *whatever is* _____

   f. *whatever is* _____

   g. *if there is any and* _____

   h. *if anything* _____

   i. *Let your mind* _____

FELLOWSHIP

Now that we have the tools, we need the right companions to share in our lives and thoughts. It is my belief that friendship with Christian friends is an important part of life. When you are tempted it causes you to struggle deeply and to have great conflicts with your mind and flesh. If you are in a situation where there are no Christians, my friend, you are in a real jam. You need to be in the company of Christians whenever possible. It is highly improbable that you will find the encouragement you need to resist temptation. Christian men and women are to encourage one another so that we might endure the hardships of life and mature through the experience. Encouragement is easily given and of great value to the one who needs it. It costs the giver nothing more than words and can change the attitude of the one who has become discouraged. We should never neglect our responsibility to encourage others. It may be that God has given you the gift of encouraging; if so, please exercise it freely. Christian friends share a special bond of love and unity of spirit through Christ the Lord. *Be of the same mind toward one another*, says Romans 12:16a. You shouldn't have nearly as many temptations when you associate with committed Christian people. The key is people who put Christ first in their lives and help one another whenever possible. Love is a necessity in helping one another.

The Scriptures tell us, *Put on the Lord Jesus Christ, and make no provision for the flesh in regard to its lusts* (Romans 13:14). Christian friends can help us achieve that Christlike attitude more readily in our lives than can those who do not know Christ. Seek the fellowship and company of Christian companions, and notice the difference it will make in your life.

7

Satan: His Character and His Goals

While it is not good for us to concentrate on the evil one, we must be aware of what he does and what his goals are. The Devil, Satan, the serpent, the adversary, the power of the air, the prince of this world, the father of lies, and Lucifer, and son of the morning are some of his aliases. He goes by many misleading names. Let us turn to the book of Matthew and see another of his names that is very descriptive and true about his character. Matthew is the first book in the New Testament. Chapter 4, verse 3, reads, *And the tempter came and said to Him, "If You are the Son of God, command that these stones become bread."* Satan is the chief tempter in life.

Satan was easily recognized by Jesus for what he was—the tempter. Satan engages in lies and deceit to get our attention and to mislead us into believing there is a better way of life than believing in Jesus. Satan dangles the temptation in front of us, like a carrot in front of a donkey's nose, and bids us to follow along and take a bite of the desire before our nose. When we nibble at the carrot of temptation, and we have allowed the desire of our heart to have its own way instead of doing God's will. Satan wants to separate us from the love of God at any cost. He will use any tool or device available to turn us away from God. When he does this, we become corrupt and under the influence. We are rendered ineffective in sharing our witness of faith in Christ as we should.

WHEN IT ALL BEGAN

Recall in your mind the beginning days of our world. Man, Adam, was very lonely there in the Garden of Eden. He was in a beautiful home, and yet with all of the splendor surrounding him, he felt something was missing. God, being loving and gracious, considered the plight of the man. He felt compassion and concern for him and his need. God in His might and majesty caused Adam to sleep and took a rib from his body. From this He created woman, Eve, to be a part of the life of this man, Adam.

What a beautiful story! It is found in the first book of the Bible, Genesis. It is our beginning, the roots of our very lives given birth in the garden. Adam and Eve were God's perfect couple as they lived in the garden together. They were beautiful and innocent as they dedicated their very lives to each other. Nothing could seemingly go wrong in this perfect place; nothing except temptation from the evil one who lurked there in the form of the old serpent, the Devil.

God having given Adam and Eve free wills and minds to choose to obey or not to obey Him, allowed them the freedom of roaming throughout the Garden of Eden. There were almost no restrictions there. The one restriction given by God became the source of man's greatest temptation. Somehow, if perhaps by chance or by the influence of Satan, Eve found herself near the one tree of which God had said not to eat—the tree of the knowledge of good and evil in the middle of the garden. While there were many other trees nearby, the fruit of this one looked especially inviting. God had said the fruit of the tree was not to be eaten at all, but temptation entered Eve's heart.

As she gazed at the fruit, she desired to touch it and hold it in her hands. It surely must taste good, for it looked inviting. Enter the serpent. *Now the serpent was more crafty than any beast of the field which the Lord God had made. And he said to the woman, "Indeed, has God said, 'You shall not eat from any tree of the garden'?" And the woman said to the serpent, "From the fruit of the trees of the garden we may eat; but from the fruit of the tree which is in the middle of the garden, God has said, "You shall not eat from it or touch it, lest you die.' " And the serpent said to the woman, "You surely shall not die! For God knows that in the day you eat from it your eyes will be opened, and you will be like God, knowing good and evil"* (Genesis 3:1-5).

Satan was appealing to her sense of reason by giving her the one thing she could not have from God. She was sure it would give her something she wanted and that God would not know the difference. After all, it was just a little thing, here in this large garden, and one bite would not matter. Eve submitted her own will and reason to the forces of wrong and willingly became a partner in disobeying God's law. Eve sinned! The prince of darkness had led her along the path of doubt and desire, and Eve had allowed her thoughts and reason to fall away to lust for knowledge and wisdom.

A careful probe on our part will reveal the truth and insight found in Eve's temptation and sin. Let's look at these five verses very carefully and receive God's truth about the situation.

1. In verse 1 of Genesis 3, what makes us aware that the serpent was more subtle than the other animals in the garden?

_____

_____

2. What information did the serpent learn from Eve? Was it entirely true? Compare with Genesis 2:17.

_____

_____

_____

3. Whose authority was the serpent questioning in verses 4 and 5? Why?

_____

_____

_____

4. Did Eve have to give way to this temptation? What do you think would have happened had she not eaten the fruit?

_____

_____

_____

Do you see how the serpent maneuvered Eve and cast doubt in her mind? He appealed to her senses of taste, touch, and smell and carefully chose words to twist and question God's commands. This allowed doubt and confusion to set in. What must she do? The serpent knew how to approach her and find her weakness. He continued on with his plan. He learned she was not really sure of herself and thus easily placed some doubt on the guiding words of God. Satan comfortably maneuvered her into his trap. As he wove his web, she fell victim to his influence, was tempted, gave in to temptation, and her temptation became sin.

It is my opinion that she gave little in-depth thought to

what would happen once she had gained knowledge and insight. She only thought that she would be like God and know the secrets of the universe. She never considered the responsibilities involved. Consider the situation in our world today. Many seek the power and knowledge of God for their own personal gain and yet never know God at all. Like Eve, they fall into a sense of false security. Somehow, they think, power or knowledge will bring them happiness and they will be better off for having attained it. Quite the reverse is true, for sin results in separation from God.

When Eve looked at the fruit with desire, certain things began happening in her mind and heart. Look at verse 6. Eve was tempted in both mind and soul. First she touched the fruit. Had it been too hard or too soft, it would have turned her away, but it felt just right for picking. Consider the following points in Eve's temptation:

1. The fruit was pleasant. It was something easy for her to grasp. Truly, it must have been beautiful as it hung there on the forbidden tree. She was lured by the appeal it had to her eye. God had made it; and everything there in the garden was perfect! There was no blemish in the fruit.

2. The fruit was desirable. No doubt it smelled good. Can't you almost smell the aroma, sweet and mild? Her taste buds watered and she sought to please herself by tasting this luscious fruit. Maybe Eve was like some of us, she wanted something to eat that would be pleasant to the taste but not necessarily nourishing to the body.

3. The fruit would make one wise. Who among us is not desirous of wanting to learn new things? We seek to gain new insight and wisdom as we journey life's road. She had the perfect opportunity to gain wisdom known only to God and to understand all the mysteries of life. All she had to do was to take it.

All the ingredients were there, and Eve gave in. Her lust for things that did not belong to her overwhelmed her. She desired things for which she really had no need. She acted in an effort to take them for herself. Lust given food to nourish it results in open and secret sin. The deed was done, and Eve acted unwisely.

Eve helped tempt Adam to taste the fruit, and he became a companion in sin. It really wasn't difficult for Eve to lead Adam astray. Women often have a strong sexual power over men. Adam followed her willingly, and he too sinned. Women, it never takes much prompting or encouragement for a man once he is drawn to you. Always consider that a woman of God does not use her sexual persuasiveness to wrongly influence any man. This is sinful and morally wrong.

Before Adam and Eve disobeyed God, they did not consider God's promise to punish wrong. God cannot look upon sin as pleasing or good, and we must be punished for breaking God's commandments. Had it not been for Christ's gift of salvation through the shedding of His blood to atone for our sin and unholiness, there would be no hope. God would never desire us to be His children. We will learn more about the hope we have through Christ later on in our study. I just mention it now to give you courage. I want you to fully understand the message of Jesus Christ crucified.

God had to punish Adam and Eve. When you read the entire story, you will see God sent them from the garden to work and toil for the rest of their days. Satan had encouraged them to pursue temporary pleasure, but in the end they had to face God.

1. Why did God make Adam and Eve suffer a punishment or discipline them when they disobeyed Him?

_____

_____

2. Is it right for us to be disciplined by a loving Father when we sin? Why?

_____

_____

3. How important is it that we ask God's forgiveness when we disobey His law? Why?

_____

_____

Think for a moment about temptation. What are your goals in learning to deal with it as it enters your life? Make a list below as a reference to reflect on the changes that will take place in your life because of this study.

1. _____

2. _____

3. _____

4. _____

5. _____

6. _____

SATAN

I almost shudder at his name. My, my, how he despised Jesus. The fact is, he still does. Satan seeks power and control of mankind. He is a very ambitious fellow, and his work is ongoing throughout the ages. We need to educate ourselves concerning who and what Satan really is. Lest you think this is a game or a fun study to fill your idle hours, let me change your mind. His work is not harmless. He has a strong desire to ruin our lives. He wants to make you as miserable and tormented as he is. Don't be fooled into thinking Satan is harmless! *He is not!* Only the power of the living Lord Jesus Christ can overcome Satan and evil in your life.

I'm just an average housewife and a child of God. I want to tell you what He is doing to me just for sharing these words in order to keep me from exposing him by the light of truth through Christ. He wants to render every Christian useless. In the past few weeks, there has been a most ungodly attack upon me and my family. My husband has had problems with his work; the children have been under attack at school; my health has been under constant attack. Satan wants us to think we can do little or nothing as individual Christian witnesses. However, nothing is further from the truth! I am not more gifted or talented than you, but I must share the message of Christ as God has laid it on my heart.

Satan has showered me with a series of physical problems. My blood pressure is sky high. The doctor has given me medication and is carefully watching my pressure. Six months ago I had no physical problems. Why now? What has changed is that Satan desires to cause enough discomfort so that I will turn away from my walk with Christ and give up writing this book. Even though I never desired to be a writer—in fact nothing was further from my mind—God convinced me that I must write. He knows I made a sincere commitment to serve Christ.

God gave me the talent and the gift to share my words in writing. He told me that I must share the Word of God in a manner that would be understandable to every reader. You see, I have no special training or education in the area of writing. But God has given me a gift to share His truth with those who will accept it in the same loving, giving, and honest manner in which He has put it in my heart. God impressed upon me that there are not enough Christians who are willing to give of themselves honestly and openly. In prayer time, He told me I must be genuine and believable to those who will read my words. God wants us to understand that we have not yet reached our fullest potential as Christians. He wants us to understand that there is some special task for us to do in His name. We must be about His work, now! We have delayed too long in seeking God's will for our lives.

Frankly, Satan doesn't like this message. He doesn't want to let it out. He is fighting me with all the fury of hell. In fact, it is hell thrown open in an effort to quench the Spirit of truth in the Christian. I feel anguish in my heart as I write. Satan cannot defeat you or me when we are in Christ. He is only bluffing! But God wants you, dear reader, to *know* this! Satan may cause some harm to my body, but he won't defeat my spirit. I have many Christian friends who are praying for me as I write this study. The victory is claimed for Christ, and we shall press on. Satan could not kill Jesus and take away the blessing and gift of eternal life we obtained through Him. As Christians we have the power of Christ in our souls. We can resist and turn aside the temptations when they come. We are cherished children of God, and nothing Satan can do can steal that away!

Friends in Christ, don't allow Satan to drag you down to his level through temptation. Those who are unbelievers, please seek Christ so that your life might be filled with goodness and holiness. Do not allow Satan to claim you as his and rob you of experiencing the joy and peace of knowing Jesus Crhist as Lord and Savior in your daily life.

WHAT SATAN THINKS

Satan thinks he can overpower us and destroy the message of Christ. Satan is a jealous creature. He wants to control all the world. A close look at his methods and his character will help us understand his passion to become God.

1. Turn to Isaiah 14:12 and read the passage. Recall that the book of Isaiah is located in the Old Testament after the Song of Solomon and before Jeremiah. What was the origin of Lucifer, Satan, the Devil?

   _____

   _____

   _____

2. For additional information on his origin, look at II Peter 2:4 in the New Testament just before the book of I John (not to be confused with the Gospel of John), almost at the end of the Bible.

   This verse tells us that *God did not* _____

   the _____ *when they* _____,

   but cast them _____

   _____.

   What does this tell you about the justice of God? _____

   _____

3. What additional information is found in I John 3:8 on the subject of Satan?

   _____

   _____

4. What is it that Satan seeks to do to us? Read Genesis 3:1-7.

   _____

   _____

   _____

_____

_____

5. Look at John 14:30. The Gospel of John is the fourth book in the New Testament. What here is of interest to the life of the believer in Christ?

_____

_____

6. Does this have any impact on how you see the world and the condition it is in at present? How?

_____

_____

Satan is subtle and clever. He deals with deception and lies wherever he goes. When we see him in the light, God's light, we know we have nothing to fear from him. Much effort and planning go into his misleading and tempting us. Satan would have us believe that he is all-powerful and superior to God. There could be nothing further from the truth. The truth is his ego and pride are coupled with a driving lust for power and control of the universe. He simply wants to maneuver us like puppets with no will and no purpose in life. He tries so hard to make us believe we cannot battle him and win.

Before we go on in our study, it would be good for us to take stock to see where we stand.

1. Are you a puppet with no purpose in your life?
2. Does your life have real meaning?
3. Do you have any goals that will bring glory to God?
4. What is it that you really do want from this life and what will follow thereafter?

_____

_____

_____

5. Do you believe that this life is all there is and that there is nothing beyond the grave?

_____

Satan makes us think, "Forget tomorrow; let's live for today." He would have us believe there is joy only for the moment. "Do whatever feels good," he coaxes. This type of thinking leads to destruction and eternal death, that is, separation from God. A careful study of the Scriptures convinces us of the dangers of listening to evil as it speaks to our life.

Look at Isaiah, chapter 14, verses 12 through 14. List the five things Satan has said he would do.

1. _____

2. _____

3. _____

4. _____

5. _____

It is wise to counteract Satan's ideas with Scriptures. Remember, when dealing with evil or doubtful things, Scripture is always the key to unlocking the door of doubt. Satan cannot ward off the truth of God's Holy Word. That's why he discourages and misleads us into doing everything else but reading God's Word. The Word is a lamp in the darkness of Satan's alley. It will show things as they are; Satan dislikes God's Word intensely.

In the Gospel of Luke, chapter 10, begin to read aloud verses 17 through 22. Listen to God's Word as it speaks to your heart. *And the seventy returned with joy, saying, "Lord, even the demons are subject to us in Your name." And He said to them, "I was watching Satan fall from heaven like lightning. Behold, I have given you authority to tread upon serpents and scorpions, and over all the power of the enemy, and nothing shall injure you. Nevertheless do not rejoice in this, that the spirits are subject to you, but rejoice that your names are recorded in heaven." At that very time He rejoiced greatly in the Holy Spirit, and said "I praise Thee, O Father, Lord of heaven and earth, that Thou didst hide these things from the wise and intelligent and didst reveal them to babes. Yes, Father, for thus it was well-pleasing in Thy sight. All things have been handed over to Me by My Father, and no one knows who the Son is except the Father, and who the Father is except the Son, and anyone to whom the Son wills to reveal Him.*

We are blessed because we belong to Christ through His shed blood at the cross. Our names are written in the book of life as members of the family of God. Jesus overcame the powers of evil, even through death, and set apart those who would accept the gift of salvation through Christ. You see, Satan always wants to overcome good but falls short of this in his plans. It will be revealed, in time, how Satan has failed at seeking to control the things that belong to God. We who believe in and accept Christ as Savior and Lord have felt the love of Christ in us in His victory over Satan's forces.

As we see more and more of Satan's character revealed, we become increasingly aware of his struggle. Nothing seems too dirty or gross for Satan to do to tempt us. His entire character is corrupt and vile.

1. Look at each verse below and describe the view that is given of Satan.
   a. Luke 22:3:

   _____

   _____

   _____

   _____

b.   I Samuel 16:14:

_____

_____

c.   II Corinthians 4:4:

_____

_____ and

d.   Job 1:9:

_____

_____

2.   As you look at the character of Satan, what extent do you think he would go to in having his way?

_____

_____

3.   Do Christians have any power when Satan attacks and tempts them? How?

_____

_____

4.   I Timothy 3:7 tells us that

_____

_____

We will, of course, study in length the powers the Christian has and the equipment available to do battle with Satan. Recall I

John 4:4. Remember, God's power is greater, far greater, than Satan's ultimate power. Satan is little more than a baby kitten in strength and power compared with God Almighty. This is why it is important that we learn and appropriate the gifts God has for us. God knows our strengths and weaknesses and wants to show us how to apply the weapons He gives us in every situation. He has not left us alone in the desert of life without hope. The Bible says we can endure through the knowledge of Christ as Lord and Savior. We can resist the devil and cause him to flee from us.

1. Look up the following passages and see what they say about the adversary. Think about how this information can help you stand against him.
   a. John 8:44:

   _____

   _____

   b. Revelation 12:7-9:

   _____

   _____

   c. Matthew 13:19:

   _____

   _____

2. Satan has never produced anything good in life. Consider this idea and see if you agree or disagree. Think of three things that would support this conclusion.

   _____

   _____

3. Satan often imitates the things of God and pretends to be godly, but in truth he is nothing more than a liar, and his works a pack of lies. There is simply nothing lasting and pure in his ways.

a. How does Ephesians 2:2 describe Satan?

_____

_____

b. In II Corinthians 4:4 there are some things we are told about Satan. What are they, and why do you think he does them?

_____

_____

WHAT HE SEEKS TO DO

What is it that Satan seeks to do? We have touched on this previously. He seeks to be God by the following means:

- Destroying
- Detesting
- Deceiving
- Terrorizing

Have you ever considered Satan's nature? It is selfish, self-seeking, and unloving. He's out for himself in all things. Contrast this with the Person of Jesus Christ, our Lord and Savior. Jesus is loving and kind, caring and sharing. Jesus listened and felt compassion for all people. Satan feels nothing other than coldness, hate, and a desire for pleasure and passion. How could anyone not want to know and experience the love of Christ and discover life through Christ when they see Satan exposed as he is?

Satan never gives lasting happiness. He supplies just a few fleeting moments of pleasure. These pleasures often cause sin, which separates us from the love of God. Satan doesn't care what happens to you. The fact is, he wants you to go to hell and follow after him. He wants to fill your body full of drugs, alcohol, tobacco, and illicit sexual encounters and to fill your soul with smut and shame. He wants your mind and body to lust after some forbidden thing, whether it be some sort of perverted sexual fantasy or relationship. He wants to have you turn toward him and walk away from Christ and the security you have in Jesus Christ. Satan has been very effective in his methods, and as the Church Age draws to a close, destruction of character is his chief aim. It isn't a pretty picture, is it? Well, it is true, and it is all revealed in the Scriptures.

OUR STANCE

A Christian should never encounter Satan without the knowledge of the Scriptures set firmly in his or her heart. Even the archangel Michael was careful with how he handled Satan's attack. Don't allow yourself to be fooled into believing you can handle Satan on your own. Remember, he is the tempter. He knows your weaknesses and tempts you in those areas. Call on Christ at all times and stand firm in your faith. Satan cannot withstand the power of God through Christ.

I think it is unwise for Christians to continually seek confrontations with Satan on the spiritual battlefield. We are not to initiate battles with Satan to prove our faith or to test our strength in the Lord Jesus Christ, but to face them as they come to learn and grow through the situations. Christ overcomes temptation when we cannot. It is foolish to wrestle with Satan just for the sake of show. There are Christians who risk their spiritual well-being by exposing themselves to unnecessary danger in an effort to give the appearance of being a "super Christian."

We have given enough thought to Satan's character for now. We are informed and are aware of his goals, and we know what course to take. With the information we have, let us continue on our journey. Know that God has a much greater reward for those who follow Him. Our outcome is much happier through His love.

8

How Others
Were Tempted

Throughout the history of mankind temptation has been a wavering part of man's life style. It lingers on the outside edge of one's life, waiting for the right moment to attack. This chapter of our study bears out the truth that all are tempted and that we must all deal with it both openly and privately. We will look at several individuals who faced temptation head on. Some of them were victors, and some were victims. Needless to say, I have limited this study to just a handful of individuals whose experiences can help us learn how to handle temptation and how not to.

JESUS CHRIST

There is a special reason for us to begin our study with the Lord Jesus Christ: He never surrendered to temptation. Jesus was human, like you and I, and yet He never allowed temptation to lead Him into sin. He learned how to effectively deal with it through seeking the wisdom and knowledge from His Father God. He soon discovered that it was necessary to stand strong and to maintain moral and spiritual principles.

I expect that when Jesus Christ was a young Man, He faced temptations like any other youth. Through the understanding and knowledge which God gave to Christ, He endured. He never succumbed to earthly desires of the mind and flesh. God has given you and I the same tools and strengths that were given to Christ. We need only seek to use them to overcome life's fiery trials and burdensome temptations.

Then Jesus was led up by the Spirit into the wilderness to be tempted by the devil. And when He had fasted forty days and forty nights, afterward He was hungry. Now when the tempter came and said to Him, "If You are the Son of God, command that these stones become bread." But He answered and said, "It is written, 'Man shall not live by bread alone, but by every word that proceeds from the mouth of God'" (Matthew 4:1-4 NKJV). These passages bring certain truths to light on the subject of temptation.

1. The Spirit led Jesus into the wilderness; He was with Jesus. The Holy Spirit also lives within us who know Christ as Lord and Savior.

2. The Spirit was aware of everything that was happening. The Spirit knew what would happen with the presence of the evil one. Satan was prepared to attack; the Holy Spirit was prepared to help.

3. The tempter, Satan, challenged the authority of Jesus by remarking, *If You are the Son of God.* One of his first attacks on us is, "If God really cared." The challenger always seeks to disprove the authority of God in your life. We must be aware that, as Christians, our lives belong to God. God the Father is our Authority, as He was Jesus'.

4. Satan tempted Jesus to display His power by showing signs and works to the evil one. If He had done so, He would have been maneuvered into doing Satan's will and not God's at this point. Surely, thought Satan, the Son of God could do such a little thing. Jesus Christ did not fall into the trap. He could turn stones into bread, but He would not submit His spirit and will to do anything Satan suggested.

5. Christ quoted Scriptures, accurately and exactly, to the Devil. No doubt, that old Devil, Satan, didn't like that! It is difficult to sway a person who knows the Scriptures and constantly obeys them. When Christ answered the Devil He spoke in a manner in which Satan had no room to twist and distort words. The Scriptures are a powerful tool in the life of the believer.

Christ used the Scriptures to ward off the tempter, and He left us an important example to follow. There is no substitute for knowing God's Word. Christ had no one there to tell Him what to say—He was alone—but the Word lived in His heart. We should know what God's Word says for our lives so that we might resist the Devil when he attacks us.

6. Christ, when tempted, never lost His composure, not for one moment. The Devil himself was staring Jesus in the face. Yet Jesus wasn't afraid, for He knew to whom He belonged. Although weakened from hunger and weary from fasting and praying, our Lord never lost His composure for an instant. Hunger can drive a person to do almost anything, but Jesus Christ remained true to God. He knew Satan was a crafty fellow and answered with short, precise answers. Jesus never argued with Him using His own words, but answered Satan using the Word of God.

Then the devil took him to the holy city and had him stand on the highest point of the temple. "If you are the Son of God," he said, "throw yourself down. For it is written: 'He will com-

mand his angels concerning you, and they will lift you up in their hands, so that you will not strike your foot against a stone.'" Jesus answered him, "It is also written: 'Do not put the Lord your God to the test.'" (Matthew 4:5-7 NIV).

Now we see both Satan and our Lord using Scriptures: Satan twists and weaves them to suit his purpose, whereas the Lord uses them as a weapon of truth. Jesus is again tempted by Satan, but still He knows Satan's plan of attack.

Satan really isn't having much success with his twisted Scriptures and clever words, is he? Jesus isn't buying the plan; in fact, He seems to grow stronger each moment. Jesus Christ never allowed His witness of faith in God and His stance for the truth to waver. Christ's testimony stands stronger each moment. You see, Christ knew Satan would tangle and distort the truth. Satan would stop at nothing to make Christ fall, if he could, so that Christ's life and witness would be rendered useless. Satan was wrong about Jesus! Jesus did not falter, but He remained strongly determined not to give in to the wiles of the Devil. I hope this brings joy to your heart. Reflect upon the meaning of these temptations and how our lives would have been affected had our Lord submitted even once to temptation's suggestions.

We too must apply the Scriptures to hamper the work of Satan. The Word of God will keep our faith stronger as we apply it to our daily lives. The Scriptures help us build our lives on firm ground. In our world, many groups and cults seek to confuse and mislead us by altering God's Word or by twisting its meaning to suit their own needs. God has promised He will punish those who misinterpret His Word or who cause others to stumble in their Christian walk.

Beware of those who use twisted Scripture and those who take small portions of Scripture out of context to prove a point. Satan did this with Jesus, and many of those involved in movements with various cults continue the practice. Know the Scriptures, like Jesus did, and understand their meaning. Read the Word for yourself, and pray for guidance in dealing with those who distort the Word of God to fill their own need.

Now let's focus for a few minutes on Matthew 4:8-11
(NIV): *Again, the devil took him to a very high mountain and
showed him all the kingdoms of the world and their splendor.
"All this I will give you," he said, "if you will bow down and
worship me." Jesus said to him, "Away from me, Satan! For it
is written: 'Worship the Lord your God, and serve him only.'"
Then the devil left him, and angels came and attended him.*

I am thrilled to share with you how Jesus reacted to Satan
during this temptation. Imagine Jesus standing with Satan on a
mountain top and Satan telling Jesus, "I'll give you all of this
if you will bow down and worship me"! Satan has tried to
persuade the Lord Jesus Christ, the Son of God, our Savior,
that he (Satan) can give Jesus something of great importance.
This passage clearly demonstrates to me that Satan was really
desperate. If he could force Jesus to do something, don't you
think he would have? Yes, indeed! But he could not! There was
no way for Satan to overpower Jesus Christ.

Our Lord Jesus Christ knew Satan was defeated. The
schemes of the Devil had failed. Look again at what Jesus said
to Satan, *Away from me, Satan!* Jesus knew there was no good
in Satan and his way was ungodly, and so he told him to go
away. Christ gave him no chance to reply or fight back, the
temptation was over. Satan had to go! He had no choice but to
obey, for he had to obey; he has to go away when we resist him
and bid him to go away in the name of Jesus Christ.

As we read the passage in Matthew, one thing should be
very clear, Satan pulled out all the stops on Jesus. There was
nothing left in his bag of tricks. Satan had tagged around with
Christ, speaking all manner of suggestive thoughts and lies to
Jesus. He used all his tricks to tempt Jesus, and yet nothing
worked.

Satan's wagging tongue and idle words did nothing to
make our Savior falter. Satan's words were empty. Our spirit
and heart should really be lifted as we consider the entire
temptation plot and the final outcome.

I don't know how your life is affected by Jesus' temptation, but my spirit soars with excitement when I begin to realize what the Lord has done for us. Jesus faced countless problems and temptations, but He stood strong through them all. The example left by our Lord should encourage our hearts and strengthen our faith as we follow in His steps.

Let's concentrate for a few moments on another situation Christ faced in the city of Nazareth. Remember, Nazareth was his hometown, and He knew these people as close friends. Turn with me to Luke, the third book in the New Testament, chapter 4, verses 16 through 30. Due to the length of the story, I ask you to read and study it on your own for a few moments.

1. List the items of importance in this story.

   _____

   _____

   _____

2. How did the people respond to Jesus?

   _____

3. By what authority did Jesus Christ speak?

   _____

   _____

4. As a human being, how do you feel Jesus was tempted to respond to the people's attitude toward Him?

   _____

   _____

   _____

5. As the Son of God, how did Jesus respond?

_____

_____

6. Do you feel Jesus was tempted in this matter to respond in a manner different than He did? Why or why not?

_____

_____

_____

It is my belief that Jesus was tempted for a brief moment. Being wise and filled with the Spirit of God, our Lord thought through the problem and weighed His words before He responded. He filled their hearts and heads full of words that did not change their minds. He knew for whom He spoke, regardless of what the popular ideas of the people might be. He told them the truth of God, and they found His words impossible to believe. Look at verse 30. Read it carefully.

7. What impression do you have of Jesus as you read this verse?

_____

_____

_____

A close look at this incident gives us insight concerning the setting and the message of Jesus. Luke 4, verses 28 through 30, says, *All the people in the synagogue were furious when they heard this. They got up, drove him out of the town, and took him to the brow of the hill on which the town was built, in order to throw him down the cliff. But he walked right through the crowd and went on his way* (NIV).

Friends, these people were His friends and neighbors. Look how angry they became! Their anger turned to passion for justice. The temptation was strong in many hearts to throw Jesus off the cliff for His words. People who are extremely angry will do almost anything without thinking through the results of their act. How did Jesus react? He walked right through the crowd, and went on His way. He did what? He walked past all those angry people and went on His way, unharmed. Isn't that great! These people were going to kill Him, and He just walked away under the protection of the Almighty Father. Isn't that a thought!

Yes, our Lord Jesus Christ saw temptation often during His short life, but He remained perfect and holy as He continued to serve God. Had Christ allowed temptation to rule His heart and had He fallen into sin, His life, death, resurrection, and return would have been made senseless. Satan would have made a mockery of Christ's gift of salvation and would have laid claim to a share of the kingdom for himself. But, my friends, Jesus did resist! He turned away from temptation countless times, and His message stands strong for those who will believe and accept it.

Jesus Christ knew temptation firsthand. He was not immune to its forces in His life. Perhaps you and I tend to consider that Christ's only temptations were those that were recorded in the Scriptures, but be assured there were more. Consider, for a moment, your strongest hour of temptation. Pause to reflect on your feelings at that hour. Now consider that Jesus' temptation was magnified many times more than your greatest moment of temptation. Hebrews, chapter 4, verse 15, tells us, *For we do not have a high priest who cannot sympathize with our weaknesses, but one who has been tempted in all things as we are, yet without sin.* Verse 16 goes on to reassure us, *Let us therefore draw near with confidence to the throne of grace, that we may receive mercy and may find grace to help in time of need.*

We would do well to give praise that Jesus Christ endured the hardships of life without grumbling and complaining. He never set his heartaches before others for pity, but ministered to the needs of others first. He never made a public show of His temptation and troubles, but He went about doing the work of God and preparing us to receive the greatest gift ever—salvation.

Jesus' lasting gift of salvation came to us because He endured and stood strong in the worst possible circumstances. Can you imagine the hell Christ must have felt as He was filled with the sins of the world at the cross of Calvary? That is exactly what occurred at Calvary. Jesus removed our sin and allowed us to draw close to the Father through His love sacrifice.

Often we are unwilling to do the task God has for us because we don't want to risk embarrassment or humiliation. At least we think of them in these terms. Make a list of the feelings you believe Jesus felt because He had to die unjustly.

a. _____

b. _____

c. _____

d. _____

In Luke 23, verse 42, Jesus prays. In this prayer, Jesus has taken a stance and made a decision.

1. What is it that Jesus is willing to do?

_____

2. What adjustments have occurred in His mind?

_____

3. What happens to Jesus from this point onward?

_____

As Christians, we can really feel the warmth of Christ in our hearts as His Words minister to us. Jesus never denied His Father anything He asked of Him. He was not afraid to ask God if there was another way the task might be achieved. If there was not, He took on the challenge and pressed on to complete the task. No matter how strong the temptation, Jesus never took His eyes from God the Father. God would not permit Jesus to fail in His time of testing and trying. He provided Jesus with the way of escape from temptation the same as He does for us. God gave Jesus' soul confidence and contentment in serving Him even unto death. While He endured pain and hardship, His soul was confident and secure.

Jesus paid it all at the cross. He taught us that love has no bounds and that sin must be paid for. Had Jesus given in to the first temptation and had sin come into His life, the plan of God would have been ruined. But it was not. God knew that Jesus would not sway. Life eternal would be only a thought, instead of a reality for the Christian heart. With the resisting of temptation came hope for a better way of life. Jesus showed us the way, the truth, and the light as His life displayed the glory of God at work in man. Jesus taught us there was more than a temporary pleasure to live for, there is happiness through our Father God. Praise God!

IN THE GARDEN

What agony Christ must have suffered before His death! Jesus' work here was almost complete, and the end was very near. Jesus was in anguish as He journeyed to the garden to pray. Locate Jesus' experience at the Garden at Gethsemane in

Matthew 26:36-46. The account in the Gospel of Matthew points out some interesting facts about Jesus.

1. What words does Jesus use to reveal the feelings in His heart? (See v. 38.)

_____

_____

2. What did Jesus say in verse 39 which helps you to understand the heart of Jesus?

_____

_____

3. Consider that Jesus would follow His Father's will and directions even unto death. In your life, where do you draw the line in following God's will for your life? What is the one thing God has told you to do that you are unwilling to do and why?

_____

_____

JOSEPH

When we consider some of the early founders of our faith, we should recall the men and women who preceded Jesus. Who among these was not tempted to achieve some gain or fortune for their own. They had many of the same problems that you and I encounter. They were not immune to temptation by any means. Let's journey through the early days of the Bible and pause to reflect on the man Joseph.

Joseph was one of the outstanding leaders of the Old Testament era. His name first appears in Genesis, chapter 35.

1. List the names of the twelve sons of Jacob.

_____

_____

_____

_____

2. Why were these twelve of major importance in Bible history?

_____

_____

The story of Joseph begins to unfold in Genesis 37 and is completed in chapter 47. God considers Joseph's story to be important. He has dedicated ten chapters of Scripture to the telling of it. Watch as Joseph's life unfolds before our eyes. Read the story for yourself and notice how God watched after Joseph throughout his life and how Joseph learned through serving God. God was aware of Joseph even in the worse circumstances. Joseph believed and trusted God's promises and applied them in principle to his life. The once cocky young man grew into a man of God, full of wisdom, who was respected throughout the land. Joseph learned the value of allowing God to work through him to achieve His purpose for the people.

Joseph's success did not come without his share of trials and temptation. He had to learn the importance of obeying God's law in all areas of life and how to apply that knowledge in his life. Joseph learned to be sensitive to God's Spirit speaking to him. This is one of the most important qualities of any of God's servants—listening and then doing what God has asked.

Joseph was taken to the home of Potiphar to work as a slave in the household. No doubt he was happy to be alive. He served his new master well, doing his best in all areas of work.

Joseph was careful to perform his tasks and was soon placed in charge of running Potiphar's home and those who served there. This was a very responsible position, and Joseph determined to serve his master well. Joseph knew God had set forth a special task for his life and waited patiently for God to fulfill that plan.

Joseph was a strong young man and likely an attractive one. He walked in the light of God daily and loved God sincerely. Then it happened. . . . Temptation raised its ugly head with a determined spirit, and Joseph was faced with a major decision in his life. How did he react? Read Genesis 39:1-18 and review Joseph's hour of temptation for yourself.

1. Why was Potiphar's wife desirous of Joseph?

_____

_____

_____

2. Define the word *lust* in your own words.

_____

_____

3. How do lust and temptation affect one's life?

_____

_____

4. What did Potiphar's wife stand to lose from an affair with Joseph?

_____

_____

5. What could Joseph gain or lose from the encounter?

_____

_____

6. How far did Potiphar's wife go in her efforts to seduce Joseph?

_____

_____

7. How did Joseph react to her advances?

_____

_____

8. Do you feel there is some way Joseph could have avoided this encounter? How?

_____

_____

Do you see how desperate this woman was to have Joseph? She was filled with passion and lust. Emotion ran high as she determined in her mind that she must have this man. She was determined to fulfill her sexual needs at any expense. The Scriptures tell us that Joseph was young and in the prime of life. Don't you think he burned with passion too? He was a healthy man, and perhaps he too experienced the excitement of the chase. His body may have ached, but his mind said, "No, I will not do this!" He did not surrender himself to temptation and commit sin with this woman.

What did Joseph do? He ran! He was quick and smart and chose to do what he knew to be right—he got away from the temptation. This woman was on fire with lust. She was so ablaze that she grabbed his garment, ripping it off him as he ran.

Don't think that wasn't difficult for Joseph. This woman really wanted him, but he knew that ungodly lust leads to destruction. He knew one moment of temporary pleasure would be wrong. He considered the right and the wrong, and he fled!

Joseph's story doesn't end here. This woman was a rejected woman. Need we say anything about a woman who is angry and rejected? She lied to her husband and told him that Joseph had seduced her. Evidently, her husband knew her better than she realized, especially since her story was not all that believable. Instead of having Joseph put to death, which was customary, Potiphar sent Joseph to prison. Had she been a lady with a spotless reputation and her story truthful, the outcome would have been far different. God was pleased with Joseph, as we know from the influence he had in the Old Testament era. Joseph was God's man and showed this by his acts.

Joseph's story reminds us to flee from danger and to resist evil. Joseph's maturity and wisdom helped him endure the hardship of the temptation he faced. Joseph disciplined his mind and heart in order that he might truly be a servant of God.

DAVID AND GOLIATH

One of our favorite stories as children is about David and Goliath. Who among us isn't in awe of the young shepherd boy who had the courage to face the Philistine giant? The story is told in the Old Testament book of I Samuel, chapter 17. When looking for I Samuel, recall that the book of Ruth is just before it and, of course, that II Samuel follows it.

David went to King Saul and claimed he was bold enough and had the courage to face the giant by himself. David did not boast and brag that he knew God was on his side, but he spoke with authority. Temptation might have said, "Tell them you are God's warrior." David's words were filled with confidence, and

King Saul trusted the boy. Saul allowed David to encounter the enemy in the name of God and for Israel.

David went into battle with a slingshot and a handful of stones. You know the rest of the story of David's battle with the giant. The champion of the Philistine army fell dead from a small round stone embedded in his forehead. David was now the mightiest warrior of all the land. Israel gained the victory, and King Saul rejoiced in the victory.

Imagine the scene around the battlefield that day. Excitement grew each time the story was told. David was the man of the hour, and he had won the victory for his king and his people. Don't think for one moment that David wasn't tempted to take the glory for himself, he was. He was, after all, human in nature and just a young boy. David had to deal with his victory and not allow his pride to overwhelm him.

Remember, this is the same David who became king and fell into all kinds of lusts and a variety of other desires of the heart. David's life was laced with temptation, some of which he resisted and some which ensnarled his body and mind in devious works of evil. David had years of heartache and struggle as he battled bitterly with temptation and desire in his life. David separated himself from the love of God by his desire to know Bathsheba. This temptation and its effects on the life of David are found in the book of II Samuel, chapter 1.

David's lust almost ruined his life. Psalm 51 is a reflection of his struggles and heartaches. When David took his eyes off of God and focused them on Bathsheba, he began to satisfy his own passions. After all was said and done in David's life, he saw the error of his ways and repented of his sins. It is well to remember that even with power and position temptation is ever present. Perhaps those who have great power are often more tempted than we realize. When David saw his error and repented, God was ready to use him as a servant and king. There was no greater in all of Israel's history than King David.

If we consider our lives ruined because of sin, perhaps we

should remember David. Our Lord Jesus Christ was from the line of David, an honor that any one of us would be proud to claim. Even though David struggled with a wavering attitude, God still gave him a life that produced many pleasing results. Where would we be if there were no beautiful psalms to read? David shows us the struggle of life and the victory too.

PETER

My favorite person in all the Bible, outside the Lord Jesus Christ, is Peter. He was a man after my own heart, full of life, opinions, and ideas and always seeking to do well and forever having problems. I think many of us identify with Peter because of his attitude and nature. He's not really very refined; he's a diamond in the rough. Peter was forever having to learn something the hard way. I think I have many of Peter's personality traits. But I am comforted when I remember that, in time, God took Peter and molded him into a man of honor, filled with the Spirit and knowledge of the Lord. I love my friend Peter for the examples he left us. Peter teaches us not to give up. He shows us that we can learn through mistakes and become chosen vessels of the Lord to carry out the tasks set before us.

Peter is the disciple who, seemingly, had his foot in his mouth a large part of the time. While the other disciples were cool and collected, my friend Peter was ready to get the job done. Some of the events in Peter's life serve as good examples of the subtlety of temptation's snare. Whatever Peter said he wouldn't do, he usually ended up doing. Still Peter was learning and trying to be a godly man, let's not sell him short in that area. He did care about the work of the Lord and worked hard at everything he did. Peter is also a splendid example of picking up one's life and going on after mistakes have been made and admitted. Also, Peter asked questions when he did not understand the teachings of the Lord. He was the first to say, *Lord, what does this mean?* In my eyes, we should give Peter a great deal of credit for his stance as a follower of Christ. Were it not for Peter's example, I believe many of us would become discouraged about our own Christian walk. Peter's life displays how mistakes are made, forgiveness received, and how we still can be useful in the work of the Lord.

Recall that Peter, upon hearing of the foretelling of Christ's death, was very distraught. He was upset and excited as he turned to the Lord and said, *God forbid it! This shall never happen to You* (Matthew 16:22). Peter loved Christ dearly and wanted no harm to come to Him. He would not have Him suffer, let alone die if he could help it. What good friend wants to see a friend or someone they love suffer for any cause? Peter genuinely was concerned for Christ our Lord.

Jesus turned and said to Peter, Out of my sight, Satan! You are a stumbling block to me; you do not have in mind the things of God, but the things of men." (Matthew 16:23 NIV). Satan had influenced Peter to speak the words that would make the others feel empty and alone. Doubtless, Peter did not fully understand what was about to happen. Confusion had begun to set in among the disciples. Had you and I been there, I expect we would have been the same. They were frightened and stunned by the events of the evening. Everything happened so quickly.

Now we come to the classic example of Satan's ultimate temptation to men—attempting to turn us from God and denying Jesus Christ. In Luke 22:31 Jesus warned Peter that Satan *demanded permission to sift you like wheat.* Jesus then added in verse 32, *but I have prayed for you, that your faith may not fail; and you, when once you have turned again, strengthen your brothers.* Proud Peter replied in verse 33, *Lord, with You I am ready to go both to prison and to death!* But in reply, in verse 34, Jesus predicts Peter's denial of Himself. We all know the words that Peter spoke later and how he reacted to the situation. Reread the beautiful but sad story of the death of our Lord. It is found in Matthew, chapters 26 and 27. What a sad setting—Peter standing in the presence of the Son of God and saying, *I will never deny You. I will never fall away or be led astray from You.* And then the events that follow . . . denial, denial, denial.

Why was Peter tempted to deny knowing Christ? What were his feelings deep within his soul? What did he hope to gain? Poor Peter is still our example of saying one thing and doing another. He stands exposed for all of us to shake our heads at and turn from him. He denied Christ! Remember that Peter's faith at this moment was shaky. He had no idea what tomorrow would bring or what God had in store for his life.

1. Peter felt scared. There was anger and hate all about him. The people wanted blood, Christ's blood. Peter did not understand what the Master had done to deserve death. "Why, who, how could all this happen? This man is the Son of God! You people don't know what you are doing? No, no, no. . . ." I can almost hear his words. The screams and shouts grow stronger as the crowd presses in all around them. Fear does strange things to one's courage. What would you have done in the same circumstances?

2. Peter felt very insecure. Have you ever felt alone and insecure? When your security is torn away from you there must be something to replace it with. With Christ taken from them, where would security come from? What would be left for him to do?

3. Peter felt endangered. Would the disciples be next to die? How could the faith be spread if they were all taken away? Who would share the message of hope and love which had been given through Christ the Lord? What would stop the people from murdering and torturing the believers in Christ as they intended to do to Christ?

4. What hope was there? With Jesus gone, who would teach them the things they needed to know? Jesus had taught things they had never known or heard before. He explained in depth things which were mysteries to men. Where would their instruction come from? Who was wise enough among them to lead the movement forward?

It is my belief that at this moment Peter was in a severe state of shock. Peter gave in to the temptation to deny Christ because he simply did not understand what stand to take. He was completely unprepared for what he saw; he just simply couldn't believe it. He denied the Lord because Satan gained a foothold in the situation using fear as a weapon.

I could almost cry for Peter's dilemma when I view it today, knowing the outcome of the situation. You see, God had not revealed to these people what would take place beyond the resurrection. Peter's faith was shaky, and his thoughts were not what they should have been at the moment. Peter had no way of knowing the greatness and the favor that awaited him as he served the Lord beyond this moment. Peter was just a young Christian beginning to grow and understand the things that Jesus had taught him.

Peter still had a great deal to learn, as you and I do, and this was his beginning. Peter never turned away from the Lord again or denied knowing Him. His faith grew stronger, and his Christian walk was consistent and true. His ministry was effective and lasted well beyond his lifetime.

Peter, the man, the rock, one of those chosen by Jesus, never denied our Lord, Jesus Christ, again—even unto his death. I give thanks for the life that Peter led. You see, if it were not for the human qualities of these early Christians, it would be more difficult for us to follow Christ. We would think we were too much of a failure to even attempt the Christian life. These people show us through their mistakes that there is a greater life available through Christ. Peter didn't allow his life to stop with his failure. He sought to find God's will and to follow that plan forever. Peter was no quitter! He was a bullheaded, strong-willed child of God. He took his life and presented it to the Lord, using the gifts and talents given him by God.

Temptation came into Peter's life, and still he grew stronger in the Lord. Although he experienced serious setbacks, Peter eventually learned to resist some of his old habits. He prayed and met the enemy head on. Peter became one of the cornerstones of our Christian faith. What a man he must have been! He learned the hard way that temptation is overcome through God and not through our own powers. Without God's strength and power in our lives, many of us would deny knowing Christ like Peter once did. Peter faced up to his responsibility and was never tempted to deny Christ again.

PAUL

Seemingly, Paul encountered more hardship and problems than the other followers of Christ. He more often appeared as the outspoken, disciplinarian of the early Christian Church. Paul, originally called Saul, as a Roman Citizen, Jew, Pharisee, and unbeliever, set forth to destroy Christianity. He persisted for many years. When the Lord changed Paul, his ministry became sharing the Gospel of Christ with Gentiles. Were it not for his faith, Christianity would not have spread to the Gentiles for some while.

There were moments when Paul seemed near death as he continued to share the Gospel of Jesus Christ crucified. Paul shared the Word no matter where he was—in prison, on the seas, in the local synagogue—Paul spoke about Christ to all who would listen.

Paul was well aware of the attacks of Satan in his life, but he was a determined man. Although Paul seems to have endured more hardship than most of the others, I feel certain there was great danger for all who shared the Word. Paul was more expressive about his problems as he encountered trials and temptations in his life. It seems that he wanted to make clear to us that the Christian life was not an easy life. Anyone who thought Christians had it made was wrong. They were tempted like anyone else and had to learn to deal with it also.

I believe part of Paul's task was to make certain the dangers of the Christian life as well as the glory. If it were not for trials and hardships, there would be few moments of rejoicing when victory is found in the most adverse of times. Consider how often Paul was abused and mistreated for his faith. Had his beliefs not been genuine, he would have surely suffered without reason. But Paul's faith was as real as his encounter with the Lord. He understood Christ to be the Messiah, sent from God, to free the world from sin and torment. Paul's life was not lived in vain. Although he was tempted and tested, his life gives us a good example of how to endure because we love the Lord Jesus Christ.

Like most of us, Paul had moments of temptation and had to take a stand against them. Paul's words often remind us to rejoice in our trials, knowing that God is working out our salvation. We are to sing songs of praise and give thanks in all things, for this is the will of God concerning our life. Paul knew that in dealing with temptation through faith in the Lord Jesus Christ, the victory was soon his. Paul heeded the instruction of the Holy Spirit and followed through on the proper course.

Unfortunately, Paul had moments of temptation that presented certain problems in his life. This happened because he sought his own desire and did what he believed best instead of listening to the Holy Spirit. An account is given of Paul's deliberate disobedience in Acts 21. Acts follows the Gospel of John and is the fifth book of the New Testament. It is the stepping stone to the book of Romans, which follows immediately after Acts.

Paul decided he wanted to go to Jerusalem. He had a burning desire to journey there and be with the Christians of that area. In versus 4 and 5 of Acts, chapter 21, we see some instruction in this matter. *Finding the disciples there, we stayed with them seven days. Through the Spirit they urged Paul not to go on to Jerusalem. But when our time was up, we left and continued on our way"* (NIV). Paul went to Jerusalem knowing that the Holy Spirit had said not to go. This was deliberate disobedience on his part. The results were predictable, and problems beset Paul's attempt to minister there. He was arrested. After a brief trial, he was placed in chains and thrown into prison for some time.

Paul had to deal with right and wrong in his life the same as you and I. Knowing God willed one thing and his heart desired another led Paul to the point of making a decision. We can take great courage in seeing that a man who walked so closely with the Lord had his share of temptation and trials too. We should also rejoice in knowing that Paul saw the error of his way and repented. He sought forgiveness and continued on in the way of the Lord. He didn't give up when he made mistakes and fell into temptation. Had he given up, the entire course of the Christian movement might have been altered or changed.

Temptation will return if we do not face up to it as a problem in our lives. Only as we change the direction of our life and detour around the problem can we walk close to Christ. Temptation will use any method available to separate us from the love of God. Temptation wants to rob us of the fellowship and joy of the Christian life. Paul dealt with temptation by repentance; we must do likewise.

ANANIAS AND SAPPHIRA

I can almost hear you say, "who?" Well, they are prime examples of Christians who fell into temptation and allowed sin into their lives. The price of their sin was instant death. Turn back a few pages in your Bible and read Acts 4:32-37 and 5:1-11. Look carefully at the information provided for us about them, and answer the following questions:

1. Whom was Ananias facing?

   _____

2. What were the words used to make Ananias aware that he was lying?

   _____

   _____

3. What effect did Peter's words have on the man and why?

   _____

   _____

   _____

4. When Sapphira came to the meeting place, what was said to her?

   _____

   _____

5. What happened to Sapphira?

   _____

   _____

6. Do you think that either Ananias or Sapphira had time to reflect on their deed? What do you suppose they felt in their heart?

   _____

   _____

7. Had you been there at that moment, what would you have thought as you witnessed this incident?

_____

_____

_____

_____

JUDAS

No study on temptation would be complete without a section on Judas. Judas left his name embedded in the history of the Christian Church. He became known as the man who betrayed our Lord. The results of temptation led Judas into a shame that was so overwhelming that he finally took his own life. He allowed his temptation to lead him into sin, and in the end it finally destroyed him.

Judas was the treasurer among the twelve disciples. His responsibilities included handling what money the group had. It was a trusted position, one which may have tempted him to want more money than the group had. Perhaps Judas had a fascination for money and fortune; perhaps it was this love of money that prompted Judas to betray Jesus. When we read the betrayal account as found in Matthew 26 through 27:10 let's think of Judas, not as an enemy of Christ, but as a man who met temptation face to face.

Judas made a bargain to lead the chief priests to Jesus in exchange for a reward. The thirty pieces of silver weighed heavy in his purse; it was a considerable amount of money. Perhaps Judas had not seen that much silver for some time; and it felt good to hold it in his hands. Judas wanted things, and money could buy them for him. Following Jesus was fine, but there wasn't any financial gain or prosperity in it. Perhaps Judas was tired of doing without the things he wanted in his life. Recall the Scriptures that tell us how these men moved about teaching and sharing the message of Jesus Christ.

Judas was like many of us, ready for something better in his life and weary of waiting. He had the necessities of life but wanted more, or thought he wanted more. Judas was tempted to betray Jesus for financial gain. I believe Judas thought the money would be useful, and he really had no way of knowing what was in store for Christ.

When Judas learned what he had done and the results it would have, he sought to return the money. His selfishness had proven to be a careless act, and the results of his temptation would affect many lives. When Judas tried to return the money the officials would not take it. Judas was so distraught by what had occurred as a result of his temptation that he threw the money down and fled the presence of the priests and officials. Judas had a heart filled with grief and guilt that knew no bounds. Judas felt strong remorse for his deed, and he knew that he must do something to escape the horror of the moment, so he hanged himself. He died a shameful death and was buried in the public burial ground which had been bought with the thirty pieces of silver.

Temptation seeks to blemish each life with some kind of sin. Only as we allow it to gain control of our lives are we overcome by its powers. Temptation will seek to fool us, just as it did Judas, Ananias, Sapphira, and a multitude of others who have believed that life is better when lived their own way. Temptation seeks to dull our senses, and as we respond to it, it slowly changes the attitudes and the course of our life. When temptation causes us to look away from God and to seek worldly pleasures, then it has a dangerous foothold in our life. Remember that temptation can cause us to harden our heart toward God if not dealt with using Biblical guidance. Temptation must be put in its place and forgotten so that we might discover the purity of God's love in our lives. In each of our examples the persons mentioned had an opportunity to deal with their temptation. They had a decision to make—either fight the enemy or surrender to him. It is the will of God that you fight the good fight and run the course He has set before you.

9
The Power of His Love and the Christian Walk

By now you have seen that our Defender is the Lord Jesus Christ. We ourselves are His warriors in the battle for truth and right. In this chapter we discuss the power of Christ's love at work in us. Many of you may not be familiar with the term *the Christian walk*. It is my wish to share with you more information on this subject and what is involved in the journey all Christians take. Most of us want to draw closer to Christ, but often we aren't sure how we can do this. Let's journey through the Bible and learn more about His love and our need to walk closer to Him.

I believe the first thing we must do is understand some vital truths about the love of Christ.

1. God so loved us that He sent His only Son into this world that we might not perish but receive eternal life. This is simple but important. Study it in John 3:16.

2. Jesus loves us. He wants us to accept His love and abide in Him. John 15:9 is a prime example of the love Christ offers all people.

3. Christ commanded us to love one another as He loved us. (See John 4:7; 13:35; 15:12.) This is a truth many Christians neglect or ignore. The basis of love is founded on loving as Christ loved us.

4. Love is from God. (See I John 3:10, 14; 4:7.) The one who does not love does not know the Father. (See I John 3:10, 14; 4:7.) This truth should make a tremendous impact on your Christian walk. These verses mean we are to love, not just a select few, not just those in our group of friends, but all people. Some of us are very select, I am afraid, and only love those who are loving and kind to us. The Bible teaches that Christian love is an ongoing action, not a convenient attitude.

5. *If God so loved us, we are also to love one another.* Those are Biblical words as found in I John 2:5, 6; 4:11-13. If you search the Scriptures still further, the idea of loving as Jesus loved will become more familiar to you. We have just scraped the surface on this matter.

I could go on at length describing the beauty of love as displayed in the life of Christ our Lord. Think of love in this way: Our lives would never be complete and filled were it not for the love that comes from Christ. There would always be something missing in our lives if we did not experience the love of Christ in our hearts. The one who has not experienced the perfect love of Christ in their hearts and souls has a haunting emptiness within. Christ's love gives meaning and purpose to life. I can remember how life was without it, but now that I have found it, I never want to be left without it again.

The man or woman who knows the love of Christ and does not freely share it is a selfish person. Christ's love was meant to be shared with others in countless ways. There are Christians who never share their love in Christ with one another, let alone with those who are not believers. I ask, why? Don't you understand how important it is to share what our Lord Jesus Christ has given? Please reach out and give of yourself in the agape love from our Master.

I John 3:1 is a wonderful verse. Turn to it and read along with me. I am using the New International Version. *How great is the love the Father has lavished on us, that we should be called children of God! And that is what we are! The reason the world does not know us is that it did not know him.* Jesus Christ always focused His life around others' needs and taught them how great the love of the Father was for them. He always concentrated on others, showing them the truth of God that He came to share with all people. John 3:15 and I John 5:10-13 are good examples of the offerings of Jesus to mankind.

So then, love is the key that unlocks the door of faith. We surely must exercise love toward one another if we are to obey Christ's teachings. This is done with a genuine heart attitude of concern and care, not because we are commanded to love one another, but because we *want* to love. It is difficult to be a truly effective witness for Christ when we do not have the one ingredient people most need—love. We must have love in the broadest sense, in our hearts, coming from God, going out to Him and all others—a glorious exchange of love. The Christian witness is most effective in ministering to others when an attitude of love and kindness is present. We need to be tenderhearted and compassionate to all people. An important part of your Christian witness is what people see as they observe you as you are, on a daily basis. If you are without love, others will notice that. Merely saying that you have faith or telling others about your faith is ineffective unless they see you live by it daily through Christ. Christ came to love and share with others; so must we. Christians, love one another from the heart as He loved you!

We should not allow disobedience in this matter to rule our hearts. God knows all the circumstances in our life and how we can be most effective in His work. We must allow Him to speak to our heart concerning our Christian walk and the attitudes we hold. We must not allow temptation to tell us that our walk is good now and there is no need to change. Each of us should continually make an effort to walk closer to the Savior each day of our lives.

I would like to remind you that nowhere in the Bible does it say we should expect to have our wants and our way at all times. In I Thessalonians 5:9 Paul states, *God did not appoint us to wrath, but to obtain salvation through our Lord Jesus Christ* (NKJV). We are very precious to God, and He desires to have us walk in a manner pleasing to Him. We have to pursue the course set before us, individually, through Jesus Christ. All the provisions of life have been made for us who accept and believe that Jesus Christ is the Messiah. We can resist sin and temptation not because of what we have done but because of what Jesus has done. Recall, no temptation will come without a way of escape, so that we can endure. (See I Corinthians 10:13.)

I want you to remember that God is concerned about you. He knows your heart and your attitudes each day of your life. He has the divine power and strength to do anything in your life that He desires. If you, as a believer, wish to know God's will for your life, you must seek that information from God. Jesus Christ taught that He came to serve God and not to be served. We are to follow Christ's example and become servants of the living God. A servant is one who cares for the needs of others first and focuses his or her attention on helping make life better for others. Instead of waiting to be served, you should be serving. Allow Christ to be your example in your Christian walk and step forth today on the journey with Him.

THE POWER OF JESUS CHRIST

For in that He Himself has suffered, being tempted, He is able to aid those who are tempted (Hebrews 2:18 NKJV). As we have learned in the chapter entitled, "How Others Were Tempted," Christ has more than His share of temptations. He did not falter or sway to and fro seeking the right decision. He knew right from wrong, and so do you and I. The Scriptures tell us we know in our hearts what we should do. Since Christ resisted evil, so should those who believe in Him.

Christ knew the feelings that temptation puts in the heart. Yet He surrounded His life with the Scriptures and applied them to daily situations. *The word of God is living and active and sharper than any two-edged sword, and piercing as far as the division of soul and spirit, of both joints and marrow, and able to judge the thoughts and intentions of the heart* (Hebrews 4:12). One of the reasons Jesus was so sure of Himself was because of His knowledge of the Scriptures. There is great power in the Word of God. We cannot place enough emphasis on the need to read and study the Scriptures on our own. Our power supply is multiplied when we know the Word for ourself. The power of the Scriptures at work in our life need not be fully understood but accepted as one of the gifts God has provided for all people who seek understanding of God's will for their lives. Since God's power is available through His word, why not store it in your heart to lift your spirits and guide you along the road of life?

JESUS' AUTHORITY

I am the resurrection and the life; he who believes in Me shall live even if he dies, and everyone who lives and believes in Me shall never die (John 11:25, 26). Jesus is the Giver of spiritual life. He takes our old spiritual nature, with its selfish attitudes and manners, and changes it into a new nature, which is centered around Christ the Lord. The Christlike nature comes to dwell within our souls, and the Person of the Holy Spirit becomes a vital part of our lives.

My sheep hear My voice, and I know them, and they follow Me; and I give eternal life to them, and they shall never perish; and no one shall snatch them out of My hand. My Father, who has given them to Me, is greater than all; and no one is able to snatch them out of the Father's hand. I and the Father are one. (John 10:27-30). Jesus and the Father are indeed one. There should be no doubt by what authority Jesus Christ spoke. He was God's supreme Messenger. He came with the authority to speak and act for God. To doubt Jesus' authority as God's chosen Messenger is a very serious matter. Jesus never lied or decieved anyone. As He spoke with them, He told them the way was not easy, but He reassured them that they would be glad they followed Him. Jesus Christ gives life anew. For those who think the Christian life is filled with prosperity and continual happiness, recall Jesus' words, "Take up your cross and follow Me." It is difficult to live the Christian life, but our lives will stay on the right course as long as we walk with Christ.

Never underestimate the influence and authority Christ had on earth. The world attempts to portray Him as an easygoing and quiet teacher during His earthly ministry, denying His power and authority. Satan's plan is to blind the world to Jesus' authority and power, both then and now. Because Jesus Christ never boasted about His power and actions does not mean He was powerless. Read Matthew 28:18-20. *Then Jesus came to them and said, "All authority in heaven and on earth has been given to me. Therefore go and make disciples of all nations, baptizing them in the name of the Father and of the Son and of the Holy Spirit, and teaching them to obey everything I have commanded you. And surely I will be with you always, to the very end of the age"* (NIV). Jesus Christ was God's Spokesman while here on earth. The authority of Jesus was given to Him by God the Father and has been established for all eternity.

THE HOLY SPIRIT

The Helper, the Holy Spirit, whom the Father will send in My name, He will teach you all things that I said to you (John 14:26 NKJV). These were Christ's words of instruction concerning the Holy Spirit spoken prior to the crucifixion. The Holy Spirit would first be a Teacher, then One who directs the heart to discern right from wrong. The Spirit would instruct the heart to greater insights throughout the life of the believer.

Because the carnal mind is enmity against God; for it is not subject to the law of God, nor indeed can it be. So then, those who are in the flesh cannot please God. But you are not in the flesh but in the Spirit, if indeed the Spirit of God dwells in you. Now if anyone does not have the Spirit of Christ, he is not His (Romans 8:7-9 NKJV). The Holy Spirit dwells within those who believe in Christ. The Spirit intercedes—goes to the Father in our behalf—in matters of the spirit.

For we were saved in this hope, but hope that is seen is not hope; for why does one still hope for what he sees? But if we hope for what we do not see, then we eagerly wait for it with perseverance. Likewise, the Spirit also helps in our weaknesses. For we do not know what we should pray for as we ought, but the Spirit Himself makes intercession for us with groanings which cannot be uttered. Now He who searches the hearts knows what the mind of the Spirit is, because He makes intercession for the saints according to the will of God. And we know that all things work together for good to those who love God, to those who are the called according to His purpose (Romans 8:24-28 NKJV).

Christian, doesn't that bring happiness to you and please your spirit? God has made all the provisions necessary to help us through life. His love spans from the beginning of time and lingers throughout eternity. This love cannot fade or diminish with the passing years. He remains constant and secure, no matter what comes. We can rest our faith upon the Mighty One, our Father, and know He has made a provision for each circumstance.

Read the Scriptures for yourself, and consider the words of love God has written for you. God would not cheat you or mislead you as Satan does. God wants the best for those who believe and trust His Word to be true. God knows the course of your life from the beginning to the end. He hasn't forgotten you; in fact, He has been very careful to consider you as part of His plan. Friends, that should really stir your heart and make you serve the Lord with a newness of spirit and love. You see, God even provided the Holy Spirit as your special Helper. God has planned a challenging walk for you in your Christian life. It is my hope that you are accepting the call of God and walking with Him to meet this challenge. As I understand the verse in Romans, it is the Holy Spirit who searches the heart and knows the mind. With all this information, the Spirit knows us well and is aware of what God would have us do in our lives as we serve Him.

We now turn our attention to the Chistian walk and how we are to achieve the goals He has set for our lives. We should be sensitive to the Holy Spirit in our lives so that we might know how to please God.

THE CHRISTIAN WALK

He who says he abides in Him ought himself also to walk just as He walked (I John 2:6 NKJV). I think the Christian walk and the Christian life are two terms that are very often misunderstood by people in general. For the Christian to achieve spiritual growth and gain insights, understanding (growth) and application (maturity) are necessary. All Christians need to grow.

Many of us, seemingly, remain the same in our spiritual understanding as each year passes by. Some of us are just as immature in faith and reasoning today as we were when we first accepted Christ as Lord and Savior. Perhaps this is why so many Christians are confused and misdirected in their Christian lives— they have not grown by studying God's Word. They expect to see things in a different light and receive wisdom from God when they do nothing to foster growth or to gain insight from the Father.

Here are some reasons why some Christians never seem to mature in their faith. Perhaps some of them really aren't believers in Christ after all. They have heard the Word and received knowledge of Christ but have never had a personal experience with the loving Savior. We are becoming increasingly aware in our churches that many have head knowledge of Christ but have refused or resisted allowing Him to change their hearts. They merely profess knowledge of Christ with their tongues, but refuse to have spiritual knowledge of Him. Knowing Christ as Lord and Savior calls for a commitment on our part; allow Christ to change the old into something new. Many of us are far more comfortable with our old selves and do not seek change for the better.

There are thousands of people who think they are Christians but are not really sure of it. To know for sure, ask the Lord Jesus Christ to reveal it to you. Ask for a definite sign that you are really a Christian in mind, heart, and spirit. The person with an unsettled spirit who is not sure of his or her commitment to Christ needs to make a careful self-examination. Be sure!

GROUP #1 There are many people who, professing to be Christians, play the game of Christianity. The Christian walk is not a game or contest. It is an intense effort on our part to grow and mature in Christ.

There are some who play the game of Christianity. Others really do believe but never grow in mature faith. Some people are too concerned with other things; their Christian beliefs are just a formality. Their faith is a convenience to them, and they never practice it. They cannot be worried with changes of attitude and heart, for it would take too much effort to do so. They contend that there is not time to read and meditate on the Word of God! They are busy with other things and obligations. Sadly, these people are a poor influence on millions of people, for they say one thing and do another. While they are righteous and holy on Sunday, the rest of the week they are busy doing their own thing. They are the ones who give Christianity a bad name. They have missed the boat by not experiencing the joys of the abundant life that comes through Christ. Their concern is centered around "self," and Christ is of less importance.

Let us focus on another group for a few moments. They struggle with the problems and temptations of life much like everyone else. But they seek a better way of living than their old way. They have learned the secret of the Christlike life—knowing Christ as Savior, Lord, Friend, and Leader of their lives every moment of the day. What makes them different from the rest? What are their goals? How did Christ become center of their lives? The answers reveal their spiritual nature.

As committed Christians, we learn many values and standards in our Christian walk.

1. Christ must be first in our lives. He must be above *all* other things or ideas.

2. Our attention must be focused on and in Christ! When temptation and evil comes, we look to Christ, not to the desire of the heart. Christ leads our lives into completeness, not separation.

3. We have discovered the value of believing in Christ as Lord and Savior. This is learned by looking for answers in the Scriptures and prayer. Then we must allow the Holy Spirit to speak to our souls. We know Christ is the answer, but we must be sensitive to God in us.

4. Walking closely with Jesus Christ takes commitment of the

mind, heart, and body. We belong to Christ each moment of the day, not just once a week. It is necessary to turn our minds and hearts to thinking in a more Christlike manner. The Christian walk is a continuous effort, we must always look to Christ as the example of perfection of faith. We have to want to be committed to our faith and practice our beliefs daily.

5. With the walk come responsibilities. Our lives become more meaningful and purposeful as we respond to life in a Christlike manner. We see life as an opportunity to serve others as Christ served. We understand there is a need to share our time and the talents He has given us so that they are put to full use. We know that all people are important and try to bring out the best in everyone. We are the Lord's encouragers, instruments of love, dedicated to following in the Lord's footsteps.

6. Life styles are altered, attitudes changed, and goals established as we allow Christ to be Lord of our lives. Life takes on a new dimension when we allow Christ to be the center of our lives. *Amen!*

7. With the new responsibilities and challenges, we gain additional insights in the things of God. God grants to those who walk with Him a certain wisdom. This wisdom is not gained or known by those who are considered wise by man's standards. It is a wisdom not understood by the world.

8. New opportunities arise in the life of the committed Christian. When we learn to serve others, we experience a new joy. The joy grows and grows as we share the love of Christ with others.

9. Our attitudes and priorities are changed. We have realized the things that are important in our Christian walk and have set aside the unimportant. We see life in a different light, having a meaning and purpose we had not understood before. We learn to be contented in whatever circumstance we are in; this comes from seeking the Lord's will first.

10. Christ allows us to be vessels in which to share the love and

personal ministry He has given us. As we continually give our hearts over to Christ, the challenges far exceed anything we could have ever anticipated.

The Christian life is not an easy one. It is often difficult and demanding. It is giving of oneself without expecting anything from anyone in return. It is also the most fulfilling and brings the most happiness to the soul, a happiness that is unspeakable. Like any other great thing, the Christian life takes time to develop and a desire to perfect. We cannot be content with consistently remaining the same year after year. We are to reach out and take a hold of the life Christ has given us, a life filled with abundance through loving and serving Him. There are no shortcuts to winning the prize Christ has for us. Building our faith and desiring to know Christ personally are the keys to the abundant Christian life. And the more we learn to give of ourselves, the more we will be blessed by Him.

WHAT THE SCRIPTURES SAY ON WALKING

One of the most interesting studies I have ever done was in the area of the Christian walk. I find it a fascinating study as described in the Bible. There are many thoughts and ideas on the subject to be learned anew. Let's look at the scriptures for information of interest on the subject.

Let us begin our study with I John 2:6. *He who says he abides in Him ought himself also to walk just as He walked* (NKJV). We need to make a careful probe of this verse and seek the information God has supplied for us on the subject at hand.

- When we say we abide in Christ, we are saying that we accept certain responsibilities.
- The Christian life is more than a claim of believing Christ; it is following Christ's pattern of life in His strength.

- We are to walk in the same manner Christ walked. Christians are to dedicate their lives to serving one another.
- We are to love each other as Christ loved—unselfishly.
- If we say we abide in Christ and do not follow His example, we are not being true to Christ. Christ looked to the interests of others first and thought of Himself last. Looking to the interests and needs of others requires some changes in our personality.

It isn't easy to place ourselves last in our own minds, but it is most rewarding. When we learn what is important to God, it also becomes important to us.

- Christ did as the Father instructed Him. He was never too busy living His own life that He overlooked God's instructions.
- If we walk as Christ walked, we are to center our minds and hearts on godly things. That means seeking to control many of our habits and thoughts. We should never place ourselves in any situation that we feel would be unpleasing to Him. If we think that Christ would not like being exposed to certain things, we shouldn't put ourselves in those situations. Jesus Christ lives in us. Thus we should honor Him in our life in everything we do. Let us think godly thoughts, and we will be pleased at what results we see.

Another important verse on walking with Christ is located in Colossians 2:6. Turn with me to the powerful little book of Colossians. Read the entire book when you have time, but for now let's concentrate on this key verse. *As you have therefore received Christ Jesus the Lord, so walk in Him* (NKJV). There is no doubt as to the instruction set before us, is there? Since we have received Christ Jesus as Lord and Savior of our lives, we are to walk in Him. To fail to do so makes a mockery of His sacrifice for us.

Remember that Jesus came to set us free from our old way of life and to show us a better way to live. When we believe in Him, we are to walk with Him daily. It is unfair to believe in Christ as Savior and King of our lives and never provide Him the opportunity to be an active part of our lives. Knowing Him as Lord of our lives is only part of the Christian experience; having

Him work in our lives is a far greater blessing. Learning from Jesus on a firsthand basis is a wonderful experience. Jesus teaches us how to deal with life much better than we could learn without Him. He directs us to the importance of the Christ-centered life and teaches us the standards that are pleasing to God. If we avoid Christ's call to follow Him, we have neglected the command to take up our cross and follow after Him.

A third portion of Scripture that is vital to understanding the Christian walk is located in Ephesians 4:1-6. Paul clearly describes the qualities we are to possess as followers of Christ. *I therefore, the prisoner of the Lord, beseech you to have a walk worthy of the calling with which you were called, with all lowliness and gentleness, with longsuffering, bearing with one another in love, endeavoring to keep the unity of the Spirit in the bond of peace. There is one body and one Spirit, just as you were called in one hope of your calling; one Lord, one faith, one baptism; one God and Father of all, who is above all, and through all, and in you all* (NKJV).

Needless to say, we should camp here for a few moments and discover the meaning of these verses for ourselves. I challenge you to look at them carefully and list your findings.

1. What does calling mean to you as seen in these verses?

_____

_____

2. Write your definition of longsuffering.

_____

_____

3. To what do the terms *lowliness* and *gentleness* refer?

_____

_____

4. How important is a peaceful spirit in our lives?

_____

_____

5. Describe what you believe is meant by the "unity of the Spirit."

_____

_____

_____

6. What is the importance of knowing that God is above all and through all, and in us all? What does this verse have to do with your life?

_____

_____

_____

Let's take a closer look at some of the important areas in Ephesians 4:1-6.

1. *Walk worthy of the calling with which you were called. . . .* Why? What difference will it make in your life? All the difference in the world and throughout eternity. You see, there is a reason—God wants to use you as a member of the body of Christ. Therefore, be worthy, show you care that you belong

to Christ. Be aware that Christ has placed great value on your
life by giving His in return. Christ placed His life on the cross
and died for your sins and mine. Show you understand the
message of walking worthy of Christ. It *does* make a difference
how you respond to each situation that arises in your life. You
are important to Christ in furthering the Gospel. It is my hope
that you see the difference you make in the lives of others
because you share Christ in your own special way. Walking
worthy of Christ is most fulfilling and challenging. None of us
can anticipate how Christ waits to have us serve Him until we
allow Him the opportunity to show us the opportunities He has
for us.

2. *With all lowliness and gentleness, with longsuffering. . . .*
There is no room for ego and pride in the family of God. We
have done nothing to warrant having pride of self and inflated
egos. There should be a humbleness of spirit, genuine and true,
in knowing that, only because Christ lives, can we receive the
gift of salvation. Unfortunately, many of us are far too busy
calling attention to ourselves and our own importance. This
hampers the work of the Holy Spirit within us, for puffed-up
pride and super egos have to be set aside or else we become
more important than the Lord. Gentleness of spirit is a necessity in the Christian walk. This gentleness is a steadfastness of
spirit, a kindness and tenderness of heart that gives the Christian a sweet and loving nature. Love is very important in our
Christian witness. Forcefulness often makes people skeptical
about the message we bear. Too often the approach has been
pushy, and the receiver of the message has not heard a single
word about the goodness of Christ. I think it good that we have
a gentleness of spirit as we share our faith.

3. *Bearing with one another in love, endeavoring to keep the
unity of the Spirit in the bond of peace.* What do we bear with
one another? The answer is very simple—everything! We share
our joys and heartaches, our ups and downs. We share what we
have and what we have not. Love is a vital part of our relation-

ships with all people, especially those in the household of faith. Spiritual love knows no boundaries. There are moments of difficulty when only love can carry us through.

When temptation, trials, and testings enter our lives, we especially need someone to care. This caring spirit is the Spirit of Christ which we jointly share with those who love Christ. For example, while I may not understand your specific problem, I can encourage you and love you in the love of Christ. I can always encourage you in your hours of darkness and pray for you. I hope this isn't too difficult to comprehend. Stated simply, we are one together in the Spirit and bond of love. Learning love is a vital step in the Christian life. Christ has taught us to love one another as He loved us.

My love to you through the Spirit of Christ comes to encourage and uplift your spirit. While it may not be possible to help you materially, I can help you through prayer and friendly encouragement. The Bible clearly says we should bear one another's burdens and love from the heart. It is my sincere belief that most of us neglect our duty in this area of responsibility. When we share faith and love, we grow in spiritual resources and faith. We can never give away all our love. The more we give, the more it is replenished. Love spreads and grows more beautiful as it is shared. There is a special happiness found in the heart of a Christian who loves in the Spirit of Christ.

4. *There is one body and one Spirit, just as you were called in one hope of your calling; one Lord, one faith, one baptism; one God and Father of all, who is above all, and through all, and in you all.* This verse says it all. Think of it this way: God has not left His believers lacking in anything. He has made the necessary provisions for our faith to be full and complete. We need not worry about all the details, for our Father has it all in hand. Ours is a walk by faith according to the Spirit.

Each of the verses we have studied has a special message for us.

We must understand the teachings of the Scriptures and apply them to our lives to make them meaningful. To neglect the Word and not study it is to rob ourselves of finding God's will for our lives.

But I say, walk by the Spirit, and you will not carry out the desire of the flesh. For the flesh sets its desire against the Spirit, and the Spirit against the flesh; for these are in opposition to one another, so that you may not do the things that you please (Galatians 5:16, 17). These two scriptures almost seem to slap us in the face with the truth. In them we see more information about our spiritual battle. Temptation attacks us first in the mind and spirit before it pricks at the flesh.

1. When we walk in the Spirit we should see Christ first in all the things we do. Our minds should be set on spiritual values and on seeking a more godly attitude when we think of Christ. If we walk in the flesh, we want to please our own selves first and foremost. Seeking to please only our fleshly nature and desires always finds us wanting more to satisfy our lusts and needs. Very often, this causes additional temptations which seem to befall us.

2. The flesh sets its desire against the spirit. The desires of the flesh can separate your spirit from the loving Spirit of God. Temptation causes you to look for worldly and fleshly pleasures first and God last. Yielded to, temptation will dull the desire to please God because you have turned your desire to self-pleasure. The only lasting happiness is in giving the Lord God the opportunity to show you a better way of life by knowing Him. I hope you understand that the Christian life, while difficult, is very rewarding. The experiences of the Christian life will fill your heart with blessings unmeasurable by the world system.

3. The Spirit of God and the flesh are in opposition to each other. The human nature wants its own way and does not naturally seek the spiritual realm of life. Its prime objective is

pleasure. All of us know that good times have to fade away at some point and leave a strange emptiness. The flesh cannot fill the vacuum left by the need for spiritual fulfillment. The Spirit within seeks to lead you into a better life, filled with promise and special contentment. The spirit of man and woman is lasting, the flesh is not. Our spirit feels the presence of God, which the flesh cannot do.

When considering your life, think on the following things:

- Christ is the answer to your needs; He will satisfy your soul when nothing else can.
- Believe your life can have new meaning through Jesus Christ. He will show you the way to make your own special contribution to life.
- Serve others through your faith and love. When you do this, your life will be happier and you will be a changed person.
- Allow the Lord to use your life as an instrument of love. You may be the person who will bring another to know and experience the Lord in his or her life.

There are many verses on walking in the Spirit with Christ. It is very important for us to apply these Scriptures to our lives and make them a practical part of our lives. Here are a few more verses you might want to read about walking.

- Ephesians 5:2, walking in love.
- II Corinthians 5:7, walking by faith.
- Romans 6:4, walking in newness of life.

THOUGHTS AND REFLECTIONS ABOUT WALKING

Each Christian should consider it a privilege to walk with Christ. Life will never have real meaning until we seek to have a personal knowledge and love relationship with our Savior. For many of us, this idea is new and strange. We feel the need to explore it further and make a decision about what course to take. Some of us need to stop and consider it in depth. Perhaps we have not heard the Good News about walking with Christ on a personal level, or maybe we have not known what steps to take to walk with Him.

I would like to share with you some personal thoughts and reflections about walking closer with the Savior.

1 Consider your life as it is. Are you completely satisfied with it? Is there something missing? Is there something holding you back in life? Ask Christ to reveal to you how to draw closer to Him. Ask that He show you how to make your life complete in all areas and lacking in nothing.

2. Be aware of the Holy Spirit speaking to your heart. Is He telling you something certain? Be sensitive to the Spirit as He directs you along the way.

3. Accept the challenges Christ sends your way. Don't allow temptation to tell you there is no time or you don't have the ability to follow through with any task Christ gives you.

4. Read your Bible daily. Although it may sound old-fashioned, look into God's Word. What new insights do you see? Make a list of truths you receive when you study the Scriptures. Ask God to open your eyes and allow you to apply these new principles to your life with new enthusiasm.

5. Pray fervently from the heart. Speak to the Lord as your Friend, not just as the Lord of your life. Tell Him you want to be more than you are now, and ask for the opportunity to serve Him. Be willing to follow wherever the Lord leads you. I guarantee your life will be enriched and blessed.

6. Walk with the Lord daily. You may only take a few steps each day, but each step is important. Stay on course; He knows where the road will lead you. Allow the Lord's Spirit to rule your heart. Push aside the fleshly desires, resist evil, turn away. Remember, it will flee from you but you need to do your part.

As we travel along the path of life, there are many side roads. We must depend on Christ to lead our lives in the right direction. When we depend on our own abilities, we will unintentionally stray and take the wrong path. The Christian life is not just exciting, it is also difficult and an immense challenge. Christ will never leave us stranded as we walk with Him. He is always there and sensitive to our needs. The Christian walk will lead us into various areas of growth and maturity, for the more we grow in Christ, the more we experience through faith in Him. As we mature He gives us more responsibilities and allows us to serve Him even more. Maturing Christians are satisfied and content, for they know they have been pressed into service for the Lord.

As a personal reflection, please allow me to share with you some of the changes that have taken place in my life. I would like to tell you how I have learned happiness in the Lord Jesus Christ. For years I did not know of the Christian walk. Happiness eluded me much like a butterfly soaring through an open field. I knew there was something more to the Christian life, but I did not know how to find real happiness.

The more I read my Bible, the more it became clear to me just what was missing—a close relationship to Christ. It wasn't that I hadn't wanted one, I just hadn't known it was possible. Slowly I began to develop this idea in my mind. I really desired to walk with Christ. I soon discovered there was something very lovely in walking with Christ. Although the struggles still occur, they do not seem as important as they once did, for I know Christ as my Companion. I began to enjoy my time of fellowship and prayer with Christ. There are many blessings in my life now that I did not have before I walked with Christ. Although I am not near the point of perfection, I am making some progress in my life.

The Christian walk is very important to our growth process. While we journey along with Christ, the struggles of the world do not seem to overtake us as they once did, nor are we immune to the problems and heartaches of the world around us.

The only difference is that we have Christ to help us along the way and we are aware of His continual presence. There is a certain sense of confidence and security that comes from walking in Christ. This feeling cannot be stolen away by any circumstances and is ours to share with others.

I am happy, now that I have learned to walk consistently in the love of Christ. I know to whom I belong and am at peace within my soul. If you do not walk with Christ on a daily journey, seek to do so to achieve a happier spirit. Walking with Christ doesn't always demand great sacrifices from us, although it often requires a few adjustments. Don't be tempted to say, "I don't want to give up anything I have now." Don't allow yourself to be misled. While today is precious, nothing you possess is as wonderful or as important as what Christ holds for you in God's storehouse. There are many wonders and treasures awaiting you as a believer in Christ. These treasures are ours because we belong to Christ and seek to follow after His example of living a God-centered life.

Walking worthy of the manner in which you were called is a challenge. When you seek to take on the challenge and the call of Christ, He will not let you fail.

10

Benefits and Rewards of Conquering Temptation

Our study has led us into a variety of different areas. We have learned an abundance of information about temptation. We have seen what temptation is, what it does in our lives, and its limits. We have also seen what God's Word, the Bible, says as a matter of instruction to those facing temptation. We have learned in-depth information on the battle with temptation and how to say "no." Our study has taught us that temptation can either draw us closer to Christ or separate us from Him. Our choice in dealing with temptation is to either resist—turn away from the forces of evil—or to succumb. Hopefully, you have decided to resist.

We have discovered that we need not allow temptation to have its way. We are free to use biblical guidelines and standards to overcome any temptation in our lives. We know, through our study, that God provides a way of escape from every temptation that comes our way. Our responsibility is to look for the way of escape and flee from any potential evil that seeks to harm our spirit. We have been given reason to rejoice, for we have been set free from the idea that we cannot defeat temptation. Where we once thought that temptation and Satan were strong, we now see that most of his effort is a bluff. (See I Corinthians 10:13.)

In dealing with temptation, we have found that often our own desires and lusts are involved. Satan is not always the key to the temptation, but he does take advantage of any situation when it arises. Our in-depth look at Satan has revealed him for what he truly is—"the father of lies." Satan leads us astray when we are tempted, because we often want to be a part of the temptation instead of a victor over it. Others have dealt with temptation throughout the ages, some with success, others with failure. We have learned there is no reason for the Christian to allow temptation to win out.

As Christians, we can conquer temptation by calling upon our Lord and Savior Jesus Christ. We belong to Christ, and He wants us to overcome every evil thing in our heart and not allow it to rule our lives. Our study has disclosed the steps necessary to defeat the enemy very soundly. If there are some areas in our study about which you are still unclear or which you feel you have forgotten, review the chapter called "Dealing with Temptation." When in doubt, it is always good to do a short review.

Now that we have dealt with the various areas of temptation and know the steps to victory, let's think about the benefits and rewards of defeating temptation.

1. How do you feel when you apply the guidelines in defeating temptation and see results in your own life?

   _____

   _____

   _____

   _____

2. What one area in your life has been changed from studying about temptation and learning the steps to overcome it?

    _____

    _____

3. What areas in your life do you still need to concentrate on to overcome temptation?

    a. _____

    b. _____

    c. _____

    d. _____

4. If you were to share something about this study with a friend, what would it be?

    _____

    _____

5. What benefits do you see in your life from not allowing temptation to have its way?

    a. _____

    b. _____

    c. _____

    d. _____

    e. _____

    f. _____

6.   How do you feel Christ has helped you through this study? What
      benefits have you received from understanding the Scriptures as
      taught on the subject of temptation?

_____

_____

_____

_____

It is my hope that you have found yourself seeking a closer
relationship with Christ through this study. This should be the
greatest gift any of us could receive—a more in-depth, personal
knowledge of Jesus Christ. There are many who search a lifetime seeking what you and I have received by faith. And it will
only grow stronger and better each day. Christ is really the
answer! When you and I can no longer function using our own
resources and abilities, we still have Christ.

SECURITY

The more we trust the Savior with our lives, the stronger our
faith becomes. We will know Christ is at work all about us,
changing situations and working out problems and difficulties
to encourage and strengthen us. We are children of God, and He
has not left us alone to struggle with the enemies of this world—
temptation and fear. He lives within our souls, and we need
not yield to feelings of defeat and insecurity. The Holy Spirit
has become a part of us, and the victory is ours over temptation and trials.

Temptation may rock us and stir our souls from time to
time, but it does not have to overwhelm us. The One who loves
us most knows our hearts. He has sent the answer needed to
overcome each temptation. The Holy Spirit very often warns

us, and causes us to know in our hearts the things that present danger to us, because the Spirit gives us the knowledge to discern good and evil. We must apply this knowledge and decide to turn away from things we know to be wrong.

Knowing the Holy Spirit lives within should be a life-changing revelation for any Christian. A part of God is living in us, and He is genuinely concerned about our lives.

GOD'S PLAN

Let us walk properly, as in the day, not in revelry and drunkenness, not in licentiousness and lewdness, not in strife and envy. But put on the Lord Jesus Christ, and make no provisions for the flesh, to fulfill its lusts (Romans 13:13, 14 NKJV). One of the benefits of overcoming temptation is a closer relationship with our Lord Jesus Christ. When we walk in the manner set before us, we are naturally drawn closer to Christ.

As we view the words of Romans 13:14, we notice that there isn't one thing in that list that should attract the attention of our Christ-indwelt spirit. Surely we can live without things that cause lust, especially when we consider their results. The Scriptures make it clear we don't need them in our lives. Frankly, friends, we have been given a new life in Christ, and there is no room for such garbage in our spiritual lives. When we defeat the temptations of life, we are, in fact, saying "no" to evil and "yes" to Christ.

God's plan is for us to walk with Christ. If we don't seek to journey with Him, we lose one of the greatest rewards we have—close fellowship with Him. Ignoring the call of Christ is like allowing a thief to steal everything we have. You see, when we willingly ignore Christ's call, we forfeit some of the blessings and gifts set aside especially for us. There are many events that enter our life in the form of opportunities to receive these gifts. What if we never lift a finger to receive and keep our prized possession? Christ wants us to serve with Him and receive many rewards in heaven and on earth.

Dedicate your day to Christ today, tomorrow, each day. Tell Him you will do what you can for Him. Ask Him to show you something useful to do. Now remember this, all of us are not cut out to be Pauls or Peters. Some of us do work that is seldom noticed by others. Don't be alarmed if you aren't singled out for your deeds. Most of us are quiet servants of Christ and go about our task in silence. Not all of us will stand out, nor should we seek to. Your responsibility is simply to make yourself available to the task set before you. Christ will cause the rest to happen in a manner that is pleasing to Him.

SERVING

I find one of the greatest benefits of the Christian life is serving others. As we learn to overcome temptation and trials through Christ, our attitudes and life styles drastically change. We are then aware that if Christ can help us through the daily trials, surely He can show us a better way of living. This way is through serving others and loving from the heart. It is giving freely as Christ shows the need.

What a blessing to learn to love someone without fear of rejection or without expecting them to react in a certain way. Christ made it clear that He came not to be served but to serve others. When we center our lives and thoughts on Christ, the importance of serving or caring for others becomes an intricate part of our lives. Giving of our time and talents unselfishly brings some of life's happiest moments. Remember we previously mentioned that some of our rewards come here on earth? My opinion about rewards is that we receive some of our rewards now, here on earth. However, we do not serve because we *have* to, but because we *want* to. Christ respects this; God rewards it! We give of ourselves, not expecting anything but very often receiving much. Often a thank you or a smile is the reward of those who serve. On other occasions it may be a tear rolling down the cheek expressing its own special thanks. Still other rewards come later on, even years after the service has been given. And at times we never see our efforts rewarded on earth at all. What is of supreme importance is that God knows your reason for serving and honors it.

Allow me to state very clearly, never serve with the idea of receiving a reward or a thank you. Serve only because you have answered the call of Christ and you know it is the thing to do. Your heart will be blessed beyond measure, and you will be a happier person for sharing your faith. Let me also say that, when I serve others, I do not usually openly discuss my beliefs. I am one of those semisilent witnesses who does not push my thoughts and beliefs on anyone. I would hope they see my faith as alive and productive through my actions. Many people, or at least those to whom I seem led, have turned away from Christ because others have been so aggressive. My call to share seems to be in just being myself and allowing the Lord Jesus Christ to do whatever He seeks to do through me. I am, of course, prepared to discuss my faith with anyone who wants to talk about it. Frankly, I don't think God wanted me to be too vocal in some of the areas I have served. I only speak when I know the Lord desires me to share. My faith and beliefs are very strong, but if the time is not right, I remain silent.

The benefit of serving Christ, as a servant, is the gaining of love and sharing of self. There have been moments when I have ached to share something of myself, but the Holy Spirit has closed my mouth. I have found that His timing is far better than mine, and at the proper time the Spirit moves in the lives of those with whom I have contact.

There are countless ways in which we can serve others.

1. Make a list of areas in which you are interested in serving Christ.

    a. _____

    b. _____

c. _____

d. _____

e. _____

2. Write down the names of three persons who you think might benefit by some act of service you might perform for them.

a. _____

b. _____

c. _____

One of the major benefits of serving others is the opportunity to experience Christ at work in your life firsthand. You will learn the joy of Christ working in your life as you learn to put away sin and temptation. What a great reward it is to serve the Lord with gladness!

REWARDS OF CONQUERING

The rewards we receive as a result of the suffering and hardships of our battle with temptation are numerous. Because we have stood our ground steadfast, without wavering, and endured the temptation, we have a certain satisfaction. We have been tested, and our faith in Christ has grown stronger. We did not surrender to the things that wanted to pull us away from the presence of God. We know that we have overcome something that has sought to control our emotions and will. We feel that we have been triumphant through our faithfulness and trust in Christ. We have sought the answer to our dilemma and have removed ourselves from the situation.

Turn to Isaiah 43:25 and see one of the rewards we receive from conquering temptation and asking forgiveness when we sin. Isaiah is found in the Old Testament after the Song of Solomon. *I, even I, am He who blots out your transgressions for My own sake; And I will not remember your sins* (NKJV). We are forgiven, and it is forgotten. What more could we want or expect? You see, this reward is immediate. Let's turn now to some other Scriptures that speak of rewards. Write them out in the space provided.

Proverbs 11:18 _____

_____

Matthew 6:4 _____

_____

Matthew 5:11, 12 _____

_____

_____

Colossians 3:23-25_____

_____

_____

_____

Hebrew 11:6 _____

_____

JOY

What a joy to learn how to overcome the problems and difficulties of life through Christ. We can truly say, *Thanks be to God,*

who gives us the victory through our Lord Jesus Christ (I
Corinthians 15:57). *Therefore, my beloved brethren, be steadfast, immovable, always abounding in the work of the Lord,
knowing that your toil is not in vain in the Lord* (I Corinthians
15:58).

Praising and giving thanks are a vital part of our Christian
walk. Christians who learn to give thanks to Christ are fully
aware they could never overcome temptation in their own right.
When we see Christ as He is, the Perfecter of our faith, our
Teacher, and our Savior, then we will want to rejoice and be
happy for the changes He brings in our lives. Our victory is in
Him and because of Him.

Because of Christ, I do not have to allow temptation to
bend and stretch me to the breaking point. Remember that one
of the things we learned about temptation was that it did not
have to be our enemy; it can be a major opportunity to mature
in Christ. We have learned that the solution to temptation is
Christ in our hearts, reading the Scriptures, and prayer.

FRUIT OF THE SPIRIT

Since believers have the Holy Spirit in their lives, they have a
special reward here on earth. The Spirit is actively involved in
our lives and in our struggles. When we follow the Christlike
life, we gain certain privileges called the "fruit of the Spirit."
Turn with me to Galatians 5:22-25 and read along with me.
Galatians is located after 2 Corinthians, which you will recall
is found in the New Testament. The fruit of the Spirit is available to the believer and should become a vital part of our lives.
*But the fruit of the Spirit is love, joy, peace, longsuffering,
kindness, goodness, faithfulness, gentleness, self-control.
Against such there is no law. And those who are Christ's have
crucified the flesh with its passions and desires. If we live in the
Spirit, let us also walk in the Spirit* (NKJV).

Each of these qualities—love, joy, peace, longsuffering, kindness, goodness, faithfulness, gentleness, and self-control—come from allowing the Spirit to function properly in the life of the believer. As these qualities are allowed to develop, they further our growth and encourage us along the path of life.

Let us consider each of these qualities of the Spirit. Write a few sentences stating what you consider their function to be in your life and what you have learned from their presence in your life.

Love: _____

_____

_____

Joy: _____

_____

_____

Peace: _____

_____

_____

Longsuffering: _____

_____

_____

Kindness: _____

_____

_____

Goodness: _____

_____

_____

Faithfulness: _____

_____

_____

Gentleness: _____

_____

_____

Self-control: _____

_____

_____

Compare the fruit of the Spirit with Paul's instruction to us as found in Ephesians 4:1b-3 (NKJV), *I beseech you to have a walk worthy of the calling with which you were called, look with all lowliness and gentleness, with longsuffering, bearing one another in love, endeavoring to keep the unity of the Spirit in the bond of peace* (NKJV). Notice that they are similar, and, when compared with Ephesians 4:30-32, they give you a strong overview of the Christian life.

Turn with me to these verses. They will help you understand the Christian walk without any doubt or confusion. *And do not grieve the Holy Spirit of God, by whom you were sealed for the day of redemption. Let all bitterness, wrath, anger, clamor, and evil speaking be put away from you, with all malice. And be kind to one another, tenderhearted, forgiving one another, just as God in Christ also forgave you* (NKJV).

I believe one of the most exciting truths we can grasp in this study is that there is real happiness in belonging to the Lord Jesus Christ. There is a peace that settles the soul and spirit, allowing us to know we have nothing to fear as we walk with Christ. Our greatest reward and benefit from centering our attention on Christ is eternal life through Christ. There is nothing more precious than this knowledge.

SUMMARY

Allow the Lord to be in control of your life so that you may experience life to the fullest. Render your service to the Lord and let Him bless your life. If you have yet to grasp the truth of Christ as a vital part of your life, consider the following thoughts:

- Christ cares for you very deeply.
- The love of Christ will not fade away or dwindle with time.
- Christ gives life meaning and purpose.
- Christ challenges the heart and makes your faith to grow.
- Christ is good. Satan seeks to drive you from good.
- Christ in your life, as number one, will give you happiness, trust, and confidence all the days of your life.
- Christ will handle the difficult situations of life. I need be anxious for nothing.
- I belong to Christ, and He will guard my heart throughout eternity.

There is so very much more to the Christian life than just accepting Christ as Savior. There is a commitment on our part to follow in His footsteps. To sum up my own personal feelings about my relationship with Christ my Lord, allow me to quote

Romans 8:38, 39. *For I am convinced that neither death, nor life, nor angels, nor principalities, nor things present, nor things to come, nor powers, nor height, nor depth, nor any other created thing, shall be able to separate us from the love of God, which is in Christ Jesus our Lord.* Isn't that a beautiful truth? I feel very secure, no matter what happens—temptation, trials, heartaches, death, sufferings—nothing, no nothing will keep me from the love of Christ. What more could I want from life? Only to serve Christ wherever possible and to accept each challenge He sends my way.

Index